Intelligence, Security and Asymmetric Warfare

Strategies for Solution

Intelligence, Security and Asymmetric Warfare

Strategies for Solution

Dhirendra Singh, IAS
Former Home Secretary, Govt. of India

Lt Gen DB Shekatkar
PVSM, AVSM, VSM

Manas Publications
New Delhi-110002 (INDIA)

MANAS PUBLICATIONS
(Publishers, Distributors, Importers & Exporters)
4402/5-A, Ansari Road
(Opp. HDFC Bank)
Darya Ganj, New Delhi-110 002 (INDIA)
Off. © 23260783, 23265523, Res. © 23842660
Fax: 011-23272766
E-mail: manaspublications@gmail.com
manaspublications@vsnl.com
Website: www.manaspublications.in

ISBN 978-81-7049-379-2
Rs. 595

Typeset at
Manas Publications

Printed in India at
RK Offset Process, Delhi
and published by Mrs Suman Lata for
Manas Publications, 4402/5-A, Ansari Road
(Opp. HDFC Bank),
Darya Ganj, New Delhi-110 002 (INDIA)

Contents

Preface

Terrorist organizations around the world have embraced many of the concepts of asymmetric warfare when planning operations against security forces due to effectiveness and low cost. By attacking infrastructure and civilian populations, terrorist groups hope to achieve limited victories by causing political turmoil, dissent, and ultimately to change a country's foreign policy without exposing themselves to the might of its military forces. A free and open society such as India with porous borders, with poor governance in some states, offers a variety of high impact and low risk scenarios for terror networks, indigenous as well as foreign, to operate and achieve their objectives. In order, therefore, to maintain national security, decision makers will depend on strategic as well as actionable intelligence to provide the information they need to decide on the diplomatic, economic, and military responses, defensive and offensive which are needed to counter them. No matter how well prepared any country is to pre-empt organisations engaged in asymmetric warfare, it should always be prepared for surprises as terrorists adopt new asymmetric warfare capabilities and their tactics becoming increasingly sophisticated and designed to achieve mass casualties. New patterns in asymmetric warfare are continuously emerging.

The trend towards greater lethality in terrorist attacks will continue. After 9/11 and 26/11, security analysts and policy experts worldwide have studied the challenges that increasing sophistication of asymmetric warfare techniques presents for intelligence agencies. In this book eminent defence analysts and security officials, discuss some of the primary arguments and current issues covered in the fields of Intelligence, Security and Asymmetric Warfare which have a direct bearing on India's security.

1

India's Intelligence Challenges

Ajit Doval, KC, IPS (Retd)

Unlike in the past when it was not a subject of public debate, intelligence has entered the current security discourse. Not only the intelligence production which can be a legitimate matter of public concern but even the processes, structures and systems are increasingly coming under public scan in this age of information craving. Quite often, the hypotheses put across are based on conjectures rather than incisive research. There are, however, many other factors behind this sort of approach besides the secretive character of intelligence work which by itself arouses curiosity.

Qualitative changes have occurred in the character of modern-day conflicts with the predominance of invisible enemy and non-state actors, high technology content, global networking and huge financed resources. The use of covert action by adversarial states as an instrument of state policy is another major contributory factor. But what has rendered these threats intractable is the limitations of state power particularly in the liberal democracies to degrade the adversaries' capacities and make the costs unaffordable for them.

Given its operational flexibility and the capability to access denied knowledge, intelligence is considered to be the closest to the complete solution. But at times these specialised skills are estimated unreasonably high for lack of understanding of the bandwidth in which intelligence apparatus operates in different settings and under different dispensations. Further, the assumption that if things go wrong they are necessarily because of knowledge deficiency or lack of its coordination is also not always true. Formulation and execution of policies and responses in the governments is a complex process and often all the options that are theoretically at hand are not necessarily exercisable.

With intelligence assuming a central position in present day conflicts, frequently disproportionate blame for failures is placed on its door even as its achievements remain unknown. Professional commitment to remain silent often compounds the matters. This per se would not be of great importance but for the fact that such speculations hamper the task of identifying the real infirmities and offering solutions. For example, finding right answers to the questions like what needs to be changed and where and how necessary for systemic improvements.

Many recent major national and international events like the 9/11 terrorist strikes in the US, mistaken assessments of Iraqi WMD facilities, which led to the US military intervention, Kargil intrusion and 26/11 terrorist attacks in Mumbai have been followed by one form of enquiry or the other. None squarely blamed the intelligence, nor fully exonerated it either. This is because there are no determinable yardsticks to assess intelligence successes and failures in absolute terms. All the commissions or committees, however, underlined the need for intelligence reforms, capacity upgrade, better coordination, etc.

In India too whenever we suffered any serious security setback, beginning with the 1962 China debacle, there has been a clamouring for intelligence reforms. Each time, as if following a well-rehearsed drill, the government assured urgent reforms. Committees were constituted and some changes recommended. As it happened, only a few of them got implemented and the nation waited till the next tragedy began the cycle all over again.

To be fair, all this has been happening when the government is sincere in its pronouncement, resource availability is not a major constraint and the intelligence apparatus of the country has been manned and led by some of the brightest persons of high professionalism, commitment and patriotism. Some of them also enjoy considerable clout at top political levels to influence policies. And yet the expected changes have failed to come about. It would be evasive to take refuge under the excuse that it is a global phenomenon and India is no exception. The fact that intelligence achievements are shrouded in secrecy while the failures are issues of public debate, the dismissal of half-truths and even canards by the professionals do little to improve public perceptions that are important in a democracy. The issue why the reforms have failed to deliver hence needs to be addressed on its fundamentals.

Reforms are driven by events. They aim at preventing the repeat of something undesirable in the past. They allow us to analyse the causes of failures, identify what went wrong and undertake measures to prevent their recurrence. It assumes that if shortcomings of the past were redressed, the future would be secure. In reality, so much has changed in the geo-political, technological and socio-economic backdrop of the intelligence missions that few of the old assumptions about why we need an intelligence apparatus, what its missions are, what are its strengths and limitations, etc. no more hold good. Former US Secretary of Defence Donald Rumsfeld was right when he observed that the challenge of 21st century is to "defend our nation against the unknown, the uncertain, the unseen and the unexpected". The adversaries have been changing their strategy, tactics, technology and organisational structures fast and the status-quoist mindset of governments enables them to anticipate governmental responses and plan for them. This enables them to constantly surprise the security and intelligence agencies rather than being surprised by them.

To deal with the futuristic threats, Indian intelligence needs to start looking at the problems purely from the futuristic scenario and work out best designs of structures and systems to neutralise those threats.

On attainment of independence, India inherited a security apparatus, intelligence included, designed and structured to perpetuate and protect the political, military and economic interests of a colonial empire. On considerations of continuity and stability, the intelligence apparatus secret arm of the Raj was retained without redefining its organisational objectives. Advantages notwithstanding, by default it became an instrumentality of enduring to protect and perpetuate the rule of those in power. This undefined but deeply ingrained, paradigm conditioned stimulus response relationship between the intelligence agencies and the ruling elite cast its shadow on its multifaceted responsibilities. It made political perspective coterminous with national perspective. In the eventuality of clash of interests, the system automatically tilted in favour of the former. This basic infirmity was rectified to some extent when the NDA government for the first time defined the charter of intelligence agencies, following the recommendations of Group of Ministers in 2001.

India's security vulnerabilities extend well beyond the confines of her geographical borders and so do her intelligence challenges. Given the size, location, historical experience and present-day global security setting, the arc of India's intelligence needs can be classified as domestic, regional and global. A nation of over one billion people with traditional social, ethnic, linguistic and economic fault lines need an extensive intelligence network to counter the forces of destabilization. India's land frontiers exceed 15,000 km, large tracts of which are porous and need constant intelligence vigil. It is particularly so as with most of the countries in the region that it shares its border with Pakistan (3,244 km), China (4,056 km), Bangladesh (4,351 km), Myanmar (1,643 km), and Nepal (1,751 km) India faces security problems of one or the other form.

With China and Pakistan, India has a history of hostilities. These countries' military build-up and acquisition of new weapon systems and defence technologies is a high priority intelligence need. As internal developments in these countries also impact on India's security like entrenchment of Islamic radicalism in Pakistan and Bangladesh, growth of Maoism in Nepal, intelligence agencies need to closely monitor emerging trends and decode the implications for India.

India's maritime security is throwing up new challenges. The number of players who feel they have economic or military stakes in the Indian Ocean region has increased considerably, escalating conflict potential in what was once a peaceful area. Earlier, China had a very small navy and did not have any maritime ambitions in the Indian Ocean. However, with its new interests in Africa, the Middle East and littoral states along Indian Ocean rim countries; it is expanding and repositioning itself. Supported by its growing economic power and military acquisitions both in civilian and military areas China is systematically pursuing a long-term strategic plan. It is building ports in Gwadar (Pakistan), Mawlamyaing (Myanmar) and planning more in Chittagong (Bangladesh) and Hambantola (Sri Lanka).

The US already has a sizeable naval presence in the area as its energy security is linked to hydrocarbon resources of the Gulf and other countries in the Middle

East. Besides oil, the US also has strategic military interests in the region. In collaboration with China, Pakistan is acquiring new naval capabilities which do not appear to be compatible with its genuine defence needs. All these have security implications for which India needs reliable intelligence inputs required for the formulation of security policies.

Peninsular India has a coastline of 7,751 km, the longest among all the Indian Ocean countries. It also has an exclusive economic zone of over 2 million km, which needs to be protected from intrusion and poaching. In addition to military threats, the long coastline needs to be protected from terrorist infiltrations, smuggling activities of gunrunners, drug traffickers, etc. For free passage to its commercial ports and unhindered economic exploitation of its exclusive economic zone particularly for oil and gas India needs to effectively police its coastline and other physical assets in the area.

From the intelligence perspective, India's security environment in the last decade and a half has undergone momentous changes. This changed conflict profile in its long term matrix has serious security implications. The following qualitative changes in the security environment need to be factored in while formulating India's futuristic intelligence needs.

The Changed Security Setting

Following end of the Cold War and emergence of a unipolar world with the United States at the apex, the global power equations got redefined. Soviet Union, India's strategic partner of long standing and a major source of its defence supplies got disintegrated. Aggressively focused on its economic and political agenda, the US is pursuing its global interests, which at times militate against economic and strategic interests of lesser developed countries like India.

On the positive side, post Cold War dispensation heralded new possibilities of cooperation and positive engagement of India with the West. The process of globalisation offered India new economic opportunities and technological accessibility placing it at a higher strategic orbit as a global player. With Indian economy turning out to be a success story, there has been substantial accretion in its comprehensive state power, enhancing its political clout and say in global affairs. This opening up to the world has also influenced some aspects of national life that have security dimensions like greater external interface with our technological facilities, military cooperation with foreign powers, exponential increase in international travel, lowering of regulatory barriers, revolution in informatics and communication, opening up of cyber space, etc. Positives notwithstanding, a host of intelligence vulnerabilities are disguised in the package that need to be addressed and imaginatively handled. For India to achieve its legitimate global economic ambitions, it also needs to enhance its economic intelligence capabilities.

The enhanced economic and political clout of nuclearised India, as also its emergence as a major military power in the region, attracts greater attention of hostile intelligence agencies and will require upgrading nation's counter-intelligence capabilities. It also has to keep close track of global developments in political, economic, strategic and technological fields to protect its legitimate national interests.

Covert Actions Emerging as new form of External Aggression to Achieve Politico-Strateguc Objectives

Wars are increasingly becoming cost ineffective instruments of achieving political and strategic objectives. They are also turning out to be high risk ventures of unpredictable consequences and are hence being replaced by "wars through other means". Covert action has emerged as a low cost substitute, often targeting internal fault lines of the adversary, employing criminal and other illegal means. These actions manifest themselves in diverse forms like sponsoring terrorism, supporting internal rebellions and insurgencies, causing political and social destabilisation and hitting at economic targets. Some of the rogue states like Pakistan have been employing them to support religious terrorism as an instrument of state policy.

Accretion in Capabilities and Resources of Violent Groups with Political Agenda

Last two decades have witnessed an exponential growth and up-gradation in striking capabilities, financial resources, collaborative networking and technology acquisition accessibility of various subterranean groups. Global mobility, revolution in informatics and communications, availability of sophisticated weapons through money has sharply expanded the arc of their activities and reach of their networks. The conventional legal, security and administrative apparatus particularly in the democracies find it too inadequate to cope with the new genre of threats. The support and assistance rendered by terrorist sponsoring states not only enhances their capabilities manifold but makes effective action against them impossible. The covert operations are also being extensively used for psy-war offences to subvert target religious or social groups. For Indian intelligence covering and countering these is a formidable challenge.

Line Dividing Internal and External Threats Blurred

Traditionally, the causes, instrumentalities, resources and consequences of internal threats were indigenous as against the external threats that they were of external origin. In the new dispensation, internal security has become highly vulnerable to external manipulations that hostile powers use to subserve their politico-strategic objectives. While the planning, motivation, finances and even manpower resources are of external origin, they are construed as internal security threats because their effects in the form of depredations and destructions are domestically experienced. The democratic freedoms, soft governance, money power to suborn legal systems, soft laws, etc. are exploited by the terrorists to their advantage. In India, while the country's democracy, economic growth, social transformation, etc. are steadily reducing threats from conventional sources, the external factor has raised our overall vulnerability several notches up.

The Neighbourhood Factor

India lives in world's one of the most dangerous neighbourhood. Epicenters of international terrorism Pakistan and Afghanistan, are located in its immediate vicinity. It is the only country in the world having contagious border with two nuclear powers with a record of hostility with the both. Except Sri Lanka, all its immediate or extended neighbours have no or weak democracies and are ridden with political instability. Economically, the region is one of the poorest in the world and economic success of India triggers both the pull and push factor, catalysing illegal immigration.

Pakistan: Pakistan, which as a frontline state during the Afghan war acquired formidable covert capabilities, repositioned them after Soviet withdrawal to bleed and destabilise India. It wanted to replicate Afghanistan model in Kashmir, hoping to make it a theatre of global Jehad for the Muslims world over. Though it failed in achieving this objective, over the years Jehadis have been playing havoc both in the state of J&K and across India. Pakistan has made terrorism an instrument of state policy and Jehadis as an integral part of its war-machine.

Acquisition of nuclear and missile capability by Pakistan through most questionable means has substantially restricted India's option of utilising its conventional military superiority to deter Pakistan. While deterrence threshold has come down, India's tolerance threshold has compulsively been increased. ISI has established anti-India espionage, subversive and saboteurs networks both within India and its neighbourhood like Bangladesh, Nepal and Middle East. Intelligence encirclement of India is being attempted as part of a multi-pronged covert offensive to bleed India. Collaborative networking with the underworld, gunrunners, drug syndicates, currency counterfeiters, hawala operators, etc. are being used as integral part of covert apparatus to destabilise India.

Pakistan has been acquiring and upgrading its military capabilities disproportionate to its genuine requirements with focus on India as the sole adversary. It has been diverting the funds and resources made available to it to fight terrorism for military purpose directed against India. Besides, stockpiling nuclear warheads, it has been focusing on acquisition and development of advanced long range missile systems. All these constitute a serious security concern for India and raises its intelligence needs several notches high.

China: In strategic terms, China presents a far more formidable security and intelligence challenge for India. India has an unsettled border dispute with China. It has lingered for over four decades despite India's consistent efforts towards a peaceful settlement. As a step toward conflict resolution, Prime Minister Indira Gandhi in 1981 asked China to spell out its position on maps with respect to the disputed borders that China agreed to do. While India had no problem in doing so, it took two decades of intense persuasion before Beijing exchanged one map with India and that too of the least disputed middle sector. Till today China has not been able to define its position on border dispute with maps of western and eastern sectors.

While the peace process is ongoing albeit at a very slow pace there have been series of incidents of intrusive patrolling by the Chinese on the Indian side. There has also been a heavy Chinese build-up in the Autonomous Tibetan Region, when there is no visible threat warranting such a step. The building up of railway line, air strips, road network and positioning of missiles in Tibet region has security implications for India.

Over the years, particularly after the launch of its modernisation and reforms programmes in the late 70s, there has been considerable accretion in China's state power. While the world has been more focused on its impressive economic achievements, China has also been busy building its strategic strength militarily, technologically and diplomatically. China's defence budget for the year 2007 stood at $45 billion, which represents a double digit hike for the nineteenth year in a row. As the Chinese system of computing their expenditure is quite complex and opaque, arriving at exact figures would be any analyst's nightmare. The US Defence Intelligence Agency (DIA) estimates China's defence budget in the range of $85 to $125 billion. In the next 10 years Chinese military expenditure will cross $ one trillion. Between 2000 and 2005 China imported weapon systems worth over $11 billion from Russia alone. The inventory included Kilo-class Submarines, Sovremenny class destroyers and Sukhoi-27 and Sukhoi-30 fighter jets. China is rapidly modernising its 2.5 million strong People's Liberation Army (PLA), which includes building up powerful blue water navy with offence capabilities, introducing new weapons systems, upgrading equipment and integrating new technologies.

Should China acquire military capabilities disproportionate to its needs, it will be a serious cause of concern for India. In addition to China's military deployments in Tibet, the country is expanding military arrangements with India's neighbours like Pakistan, Myanmar, Sri Lanka, Bangladesh, Maldives and the Seychelles. This strategic encirclement has serious implications for India. China is also developing ports with military capabilities in Gwadar, Pakistan, Mawlamyaing, Myanmar and plans for one at Chittagong in Bangladesh. Though strategic and matters of military interest will be India's primary intelligence requirements, the technology advancements, presence in Indian Ocean region and military and economic cooperation with other countries of the region will have to remain on intelligence focus.

Bangladesh: In Bangladesh, extremist Islamic group of the Jehadi variety have mushroomed and entrenched themselves. Notable among them being Harkat-Ul-Jehad Islami (HUJI), Jamat-ul-Mujahideen, Harkat-ul-Ansar, Chhatra Shibir, etc. The development seriously militates against India's security interests. Following the September 2001 crackdown by the West in Afghanistan against Taliban and al-Qaeda activists, a good number of them escaped for safety to Bangladesh with the tacit support of the ISI. The local fundamentalist groups, connived by Bangladesh intelligence agencies, provided them shelter. Over the years, Bangladesh has emerged as an important base of Islamic terrorists and in a large number of terrorist attacks mounted against India, Bangladesh soil has been used. It has also been an important transit route for the terrorists and smuggling of weapons and explosives into India. The activities of Islamic militants in North East have also been on a sharp increase.

With impunity Bangladesh has been providing safe sanctuaries to North East insurgent groups, particularly ULFA and NDFB of Assam, NSCN(IM) of Nagaland and NLFT of Tripura. The intensity of demographic invasion from Bangladesh has also assumed serious proportions and the number of illegal migrants are now estimated to be above two crore. While earlier the bordering states of North East, West Bengal and Bihar were the worst affected, the illegal immigrants have now found their way into many interior parts of the country, including UP, Maharashtra, Orissa and Delhi. The policing and intelligence coverage of 4,351 km border large stretches of which are highly porous and treacherous poses a serious intelligence and security challenge. The other area of concern for India is the increasing defence cooperation between Bangladesh and China. This cooperation has strategic import for India, particularly in the context of India's security interests in the Indian Ocean.

Internal Security

In today's world, Internal Security has emerged as an area of primordial security concern for three reasons. Firstly, in post- Second World War period most of the states have suffered degradation, destabilisation or disintegration more due to internal than external factors. Secondly, internal fault lines are increasingly being used by the hostile powers to achieve their political and strategic objectives as wars are becoming unaffordably high cost ventures with unpredictable consequences. Thirdly, the internal violent groups have acquired technologies, fire power, trans-national linkages and financial resources that seriously threaten national sovereignty, integrity and stability. India with its large and diverse population, social and economic fault lines, a free democratic system with weak governing structures faces a large number of internal security problems. They are compounded by hostile covert actions by neighbours like Pakistan. Securing the country internally from the destabilising and disintegrating forces poses a serious challenge to intelligence agencies.

Among the internal security threats, terrorism constitutes the most formidable challenge. Besides Pakistan's active sponsorship of Jehadi groups, their pernicious ideology access to sophisticated weapons, state-of-the-art communication equipments, high degree of skills and motivation, financial resources, etc. have given unprecedented strength to these groups. The emergence of suicide attacks have increased manifold the destructive potential of the scourge.

Global resurgence of Islamic radicalism and growth of Jehadi Wahabism poses a serious security and ideological threat given India's big Muslim population on one hand and its being flanked by two Islamic countries where radical Islam is in sharp ascendancy on the other.

A large number of youth both Pakistani and Indian trained by the ISI and disguised as Indian citizens have been strategically positioned as part of an intricately networked covert apparatus. Mushrooming of Madrassas and Islamic institutions in large numbers propagating an ideology of hate and exclusiveness, particularly in the border areas, is sinister. Collaborative networking with the underworld, gunrunners, drug syndicates, currency counterfeiters, hawala operators, border couriers, etc., are being used as integral part of covert apparatus to destabilise India. The conventional responses are increasingly proving inadequate in the wake of their global reach, money power, political linkages and ability to suborn the system.

The role of intelligence in combating terrorism will have to be both knowledge extensive and operation intensive. The intelligence agencies will have to develop data-banks in respect of terrorist organisations, their ideology, structural hierarchy, collaborative linkages including with overground groups and individuals, sources of finances, weapons procurement, etc. At operation level they should develop capabilities to know about their future plans, new tactics and methodology, assumed identity and alibi, communication channels and codes, personality details and weaknesses of their major operatives. Intelligence will have to operate at proactive level to degrade their capabilities, at preventive level to support security agencies on protective duties and at investigational level to help the investigating agencies in tracking the culprits and gather evidence against them. They will also have to develop high technical capabilities and their innovative use to outsmart the terrorists.

Left Wing Extremism

Inexorable growth of Left Wing extremism in the country's hinterland is another area of grave security concern. It has the potential of spreading fast and undermining India's democracy, constitution, rule of law and social harmony. In recent years, there has been fast accretion in their spatial growth, strength of armed cadres, weapon acquisitions and militarisation of the movement, ability to raise funds, recruitment and increase in fire power. Their ability to mobilise public support and challenge the writ of the lawfully established government by holding Jan Adalats, collecting taxes, and dispensing justice are causes of serious concern. High grade Intelligence capability, both for strategic planning and tactical actions, would be necessary to counter their growing menace.

North-East

From security point of view North-East is the most vulnerable geographical region of the country. Out of its total 5,132 km long border nearly 99.5 per cent is international border and is connected to the Indian mainland by a narrow corridor known as Chicken Neck. Except Bhutan, with which India shares nearly 800 km of border, with all the other countries i.e China, Bangladesh and Myanmar it faces one or the other security related problems. Forty per cent of its 3.2 crore population is inhabited by nearly 200 tribes and sub-tribes which for centuries have remained insulated from the national mainstream. Tribal xenophobia and inter-tribal rivalries have given a rise to various brands of insurgencies that had affected almost all the states of the region. Economic backwardness, weak administrative infrastructure and poor communications have compounded its security problems.

The foreign bases of North-Eastern insurgents in Bangladesh and Myanmar, are today the main sustaining factors of insurgencies in the North-East. Political demands that worked as initiator of insurgencies have taken a back seat with dwindling public support and limited armed capabilities of the insurgents against the might of Indian state. In addition to the safe heavens, the adjoining countries are being used by insurgents to smuggle weapons, impart training and use as transit routes. One of the strategic considerations for Bangladesh to provide sanctuaries to them is the advantage it provides in pushing illegal immigrants to India as it makes it difficult for the insurgents to direct their anti outsider agenda against the Bangladeshis. Moreover, it focuses the attention of Security

Forces to insurgent activities thereby reducing the pressure on the illegal immigrants. To cope with the security challenges in the North-East, both from internal and external threats, intelligence infrastructure in the region will have to be strengthened substantially.

Technology

Technology upgrade and integration by the intelligence agencies will be one of the major futuristic requirements of Indian intelligence. Unlike other areas, most of the sophisticated intelligence technologies fall in denied areas and cannot be easily obtained from external sources. For reasons of security, the R&D tasks cannot be allocated to research institutions which do not adhere to required level of security insulation. The agencies themselves do not have the elaborate infrastructure and trained manpower which can undertake high precision research projects. However, country has technological capabilities of high order in various advanced areas, with which suitable modifications can be improvised for intelligence applications. Some of the commercially high technologies available abroad can be imported and integrated with required modifications. A specialised technical intelligence agency was created in 2003 by the government to meet diverse high technology requirements of the intelligence agencies. It needs to be given the entire boost and as being a capital intensive venture; the works should not suffer for want of adequate financial resources.

Lack of coordination is often blamed for many intelligence failures. However, intelligence being a highly sensitive and multilayered activity with diverse consumer requirements, perfect coordination as a concept is faulty and as a goal non-achievable. What should be attempted is a system based convergence at different levels on a need-to-know basis. Convergence is an inbuilt system integration, as part of the process itself, whereas coordination is an outside effort to combine two or more de-partite elements through an institutional or individual effort. While coordination is a deliberate independent activity, convergence is automated. Instead of convergence we inadvertently encouraged divergence by splitting the intelligence bureau into IB and RAW and allowing mushrooming of intelligence outfits with ill-defined objectives and nebulous accountability. This has led to lack of synergy, communication gaps and the nation is deprived of making optimal use of its knowledge reservoir and intelligence assets. New systems encouraging convergence at tactical, strategico-tactical and strategic levels need to be evolved.

India lives in a troubled neighbourhood which impacts both on its internal and external security. This is likely to continue necessitating a synergised intelligence strategy for our neighbourhood. Conventionally, the causes, instrumentalities and resources of internal threats have been indigenous. It no more holds good. Today, internal security is highly vulnerable to external stimulants whose politico-strategic objectives, planning, motivation, finances and resources, all are of external origin. Technological upgrade and integration will be one of the major futuristic requirements of Indian intelligence. To meet these challenges what Indian intelligence needs is transformation and not reformation. The construct of reforms is of identifying and redressing the past errors. Transformation is bringing about changes focusing on the future. We need to identify our intelligence needs, prioritise them and plan a structure to achieve the laid down objective under a time bound programme. In fact, what is essentially required is a paradigm shift vis-a-vis intelligence operations.

2

Nuclear Terrorism: An Overview

General S Padmanabhan, PVSM, AVSM, VSM, (Retd)

Terrorism may be defined as the deliberate use of force against non-combatant targets by groups of persons or clandestine agencies. The motivation of the terrorist may be political, ideological, religious or some personal aggrandizement. Whenever terrorism involves the citizens or the territory of more than one country it is known as 'international terrorism' and the group or groups practising such an activity are called 'international terrorists'.

Terrorism has been a part of human history from its earliest days. It certainly did not originate on 11th September, 2001, though the 9/11 event, as it has come to be known, was one of the most ghastly examples of international terrorism. So far, the world has been fortunate that it has not experienced nuclear terrorism even though at least one self-aborted attempt did take place in Russia on November 23, 1995.

The aim of terrorists is to influence the mind of the target population by actions that will inspire terror, panic and despair; reduce target governments to a state of helplessness, confusion and ill-considered actions. Ultimately, the terrorists expect to be able to force the target population/government to obey the terrorists' dictates and accede to their demands.

All firearms, portable rockets, explosive devices ranging from grenades to large landmines, gases and incendiary agents of various types have been used by terrorists so far. With weapons of mass destruction (WMD) like nuclear, chemical, biological and radiological weapons now within their reach, we should expect terrorists to use these as well.

International Terrorist Organisations

Four types of international terrorist organisations can be identified. These are:

State sponsored Groups: These are groups which the government of the state, usually through its external intelligence agency, sponsors, aids and abets in their terrorist activities in other states. The sponsoring states generally find their names listed in the US list of 'rogue' states with some selective exclusions as in the case of Pakistan. These groups are given comprehensive support by their sponsor state, generally covertly.

Non-State Groups: These are 'home' grown groups with their own political agendas but are not international in their terrorist activities except for raising funds and purchasing weapons. India's People's War Group and the recently demised LTTE may be clubbed under this head.

State-run Groups: These are directly organized, administered, and directed by the state itself. Usually small, they constitute an extra-legal extension of the state's intelligence apparatus and are used for specific missions abroad including selective assassinations, sabotage, kidnapping and so on. Israel, Iran, Pakistan, North Korea and even some advanced countries operate such groups.

Terrorist States: These are exceptional cases wherein a state in its own right earns the label of being 'terrorist' by carrying out actions both against its own citizens and those of other countries. Taliban ruled Afghanistan was one such state. A number of Central African countries could also qualify for this dubious title.

Fellow-Travellers: Terrorist organizations extensively use many groups of people who operate outside the law such as drug mafias, clandestine arms merchants, moneylenders and 'hawala' operators, hoarders, black-marketeers, forgers and many others with a criminal background. These fellow-travellers are not generally 'organised' but perform useful services for the organization. One category must be specially singled out of this group, i.e. religious or quasi-religious persons whose aim is to see that their form of religion supplants all others in the country they are operating in.

So far, our discussion has been about international terrorism and terrorist groups in general. Let us now focus on how international terrorist groups may plan to employ nuclear weapons or radiological materials.

Nuclear Terrorism

After the USA attacked Hiroshima and Nagasaki with atom bombs in August, 1945, no country has employed nuclear weapons against an adversary in the numerous wars that have been fought over the past 64 years.

However, the world's combined nuclear stockpile including both atom and hydrogen bombs, has multiplied to approximately 70,000 bombs – enough to destroy our planet. Despite availability in abundance, if nuclear weapons have not been used in action since 1945, one may be rightly tempted to conclude that they are not usable in war. Yet, the threat of use of a nuclear weapon by anyone against anyone else, inspires the world with a sense of horror and terror. And terror is the 'stock in trade' of an international terrorist; he is quite capable of using an atom bomb to add force to a demand. The nineteenth century Russian anarchist Kropotkin, who espoused the cause of mass terrorism, enunciated the basic principle of modern terrorism : "Do it with bombs", he said. Perhaps, we may yet see a terrorist group use the threat of a nuclear weapon or the weapon itself to secure its objectives. Retribution will, without doubt, be visited on the terrorist group, but they will have to be first found before they can be destroyed. The much vaunted 'second strike capability' of nuclear powers is, therefore, unlikely to discourage a terrorist group from using its bomb. Groups such as al-Qaeda, Hamas, Hezbollah, Aum Shinsi Kyo and the Lashkar-e-Taiba are all unscrupulous enough to use nuclear weapons to achieve their end. But before reaching the stage of nuclear terrorism, they will need wherewithal to give meaning to the nuclear threats. Let us see what possible nuclear weapons they could hope to acquire for their nefarious purposes.

Nuclear Weapons/Materials for Terrorism

One or more of the following three types of nuclear materials may be of use to the intending nuclear terrorist organizations:

(a) An intact, fully serviceable nuclear bomb together with connected delivery system and codes controlling the launching, arming and detonation of the weapon. It is most unlikely that a terrorist organization can obtain these items. A terrorist state, may, however have a fair chance of either developing her own arsenal or obtaining these from a like-minded state or steal from a nuclear power which is so lax as to allow the theft of these deadly items. One such loss of intact Soviet 'Suitcase Bombs' is reported to have actually happened during the period the USSR was in the process of splitting up into many independent states. The evidence comes from the lips of both Osama bin Laden and his Deputy Dr Ayman al Zawahiri who, in a 2001 interview with Hamid Mir, a Pakistani journalist, clearly stated that al-Qaeda had obtained through the agency of Chechen rebels, 20 "Suitcase Bombs" each weighing about 30 kg and on detonation, capable of producing a yield of 0.5 to 1 kiloton. These bombs are worn like backpacks or carried like a smart suitcase and presumably they are not overly burdened with control codes and locks etc. Some corroboration of this al-Qaeda statement can be found in the 1997 statement of Russian General Alexander Lebed, then National Security Assistant to Boris Yeltsin. He reported that 84 suitcase bombs ('Yadernyi ranets') could not be accounted for by them.

As a matter of interest, al-Qaeda is said to have paid for the 20 suitcase bombs in the form of $30 million in cash and two tons of refined heroin from laboratories located in Afghanistan (then valued at about $700 million).

(b) Fissile materials and/or components of nuclear bombs which could be put together to produce a functioning weapon. On the face of it, it seems as difficult a proposition as stealing a functioning atom bomb. Unfortunately, data published in the report of the project commissioned by the Nuclear Age Peace Foundation, suggests that substantial quantities of fissile materials have been systematically spirited away by mostly unknown parties since the late 1950s till end 1994, the period for which the report could be accessed from the Internet at nuclearfiles.org. The USA and the then USSR have been the 'losers' of nuclear material while Israel figures fairly regularly as the presumed beneficiary.

The list goes on and on involving nuclear weapons laboratories in Russia, Russian naval and research reactors and suggests that neither the USA nor the USSR were vigilant enough about the theft of nuclear materials.

(c) Low grade nuclear materials could be obtained from hospitals (radiation therapy units, diagnostic and research facilities), industrial and construction sites and so on. Materials such as cesium-137, cobalt-60, iridium-192 and strontium-90 (from Russian built radio-thermal generators). These materials, though metallic, get dispersed as a mixture of oxides and nitrates when they are packed with a conventional explosive and detonated. This is what is called a 'Dirty Bomb'.

Fabrication of a Nuclear Bomb/Radiological Dispersal Device (RDD)

The basic technology for making atom bombs is freely available. However, fabricating bombs from fissile material randomly acquired and of dubious provenance, is a very different matter. We could call a bomb so fabricated as an improvised nuclear device (IND) – rather like IEDs one is so familiar with from our counter-insurgency experiences. The INDs are most unlikely to have hemispherical cores as this design requires multiple, simultaneous detonations to reach critical mass. The USA's Mark 5 A-Bomb has 92 detonation points. It is, therefore, more likely that INDs will be 'gun type' weapons using uranium (U-235) with about 50 kg of highly enriched uranium (HEU) rather than a complex, implosion type weapon using plutonium (PU-239). These INDs are unlikely to have fail-safe features of military bombs and rigid protocols to control their arming and eventual detonation.

The RDD or 'Dirty Bomb' is a relatively crude affair. It is assembled by packing together in a mixture 30-35 kg of an explosive like dynamite and a radioactive material, say caesium (Cs-137) in a suitable container with arrangements to either remotely detonate the mixture by electronic signal or by timer or any other manner. The explosion of an RDD would cause physical damage to property near the explosion site due to the dynamite, perhaps within a distance of a city block. There would be radiation-induced skin injuries, say up to 2 to 3 city blocks and general radiological contamination over a wider distance.

Terrorists' Nuclear Threat

Scenario 1: The detonation of an al-Qaeda 'Suitcase Bomb' at rush hour on Times Square in New York, may produce a yield of one kiloton. It will cause widespread destruction, deaths and injuries like any other small yield A-Bomb. The reaction of the USA will, predictably be violent and vicious. All known locations of al-Qaeda's leadership would be struck by 5 to 20 kiloton nuclear bombs delivered by missiles launched from submarines. The reprisal nuclear attacks may be repeated at different places in Afghanistan and along the Pakistan-Afghan border. There will be enormous loss of innocent lives. Al-Qaeda leadership may be killed or may live to fight another day. What has al-Qaeda achieved by its first suitcase bomb attack? It would seem that the terrorist organization has lost the sympathy of people who were earlier for them in the USA, all of Afghanistan and Pakistan for the killing of innocents brought upon themselves by the al-Qaeda action. Al-Qaeda may not have a friend left anywhere in the world. This scenario suggests that such an attack may not be initiated by al-Qaeda.

Scenario 2: Frustrated by lack of results in their war on terror and sensing that her NATO allies are withdrawing their forces and soon the USA would be alone in the field with Pakistan, the USA decides on the basis of what they assess as an accurate and timely piece of intelligence about a meeting of al-Qaeda leadership in Jalalabad, to carry out a nuclear attack on the city with a 20 kiloton high air burst following a drone-directed missile attack on the venue of the al-Qaeda meeting. No warning was to be given to the people of Jalalabad in the interest of achieving surprise! The attack is delivered. Over 18000 citizens died and Jalalabad ceased to be habitable. Six hours after this terrible tragedy, two suitcase bombs each were detonated by al-Qaeda 'moles' in Washington DC, New York, Chicago, Los Angeles and San Francisco. The detonation in San Francisco was followed by an earthquake of magnitude 8 on the Richter scale adding to the overall effect of the al-Qaeda strike. Over 90,000 US citizens were killed and more than three times the number injured. What did the USA and al-Qaeda achieve by their respective actions? The USA, to put it simply, had committed a mass murder due to its frustration at lack of results in its war on terror. They may expect no sympathy from any part of the Muslim world and from over 90 per cent of other countries. They have, in effect, scored a goal against themselves. Al-Qaeda will seek to explain its reaction as being in accordance with their stated policy of 'an eye for an eye....' And in any case argue that they did not initiate the nuclear exchanges. They will be hated comprehensively in the USA, but elsewhere, their stock would rise. More young Muslims and many youth from other faiths will seek to join their 'jihad'. The USA, clearly, is a loser on all counts.

Likelihood of a Terrorist Nuclear Attack: In the two scenarios we have examined, first use of a nuclear bomb appears to be counterproductive – whether by the terrorist group or by the USA. In the second 'strike' the terrorist secures the honours though he has lost a major city and some, if not all, of his leadership. An explosive first strike by a terror group or by their opponents seems ill-advised and hence is unlikely. On the other hand, the use of RDD in the form of a dirty bomb could pay some dividends to the terror group, as such an attack cannot invite an unrestrained nuclear second strike. It is, therefore, considered more likely that an RDD attack may occur at some stage, provided the terrorists have prepositioned their 'dirty bombs' and have ensured that they are secure and that the radioactive material is still potent enough to cause the desired level of radiation burns and general contamination. Even in the case of an RDD attack, it would be foolish on the part of the terrorist group to use it in the 'first strike'. Even in this case, it should remain only as a second strike contingency – as a response to a nuclear attack and calibrated in proportion to the damage they had suffered.

Nuclear Terrorists' targets: We referred earlier to a self-aborted RDD attack that took place on 23 November 1995 in Moscow, Russia. Chechen rebels had fabricated a 'dirty bomb' by packing together a mixture of about 30 kg of cesium (Cs-137) and dynamite. This they positioned in Moscow's Ismailovsky Park. However, they decided not to detonate the RDD but instead informed the national TV station so that all Russia may know they have been spared by the Chechens – a moral victory. This is one kind of nuclear target. Other targets could be major population centres, commercial hubs, major communication centres and, possibly religious places – specially Jewish or Hindu. Nuclear facilities are also likely targets, but successfully attacking them is very difficult. Terrorists are likely to exclude areas initiated by their co-religionists.

Countermeasures against Nuclear Terrorism

Terrorism of any nature is born out of the circumstances, hopes, aspirations, frustrations and hatreds that have incubated over countless years in the hearts of individuals and groups of people. Feelings long suppressed, break out under certain conditions as terrorism. A popular government, which cares for all classes of people, is responsive to their needs and is perceived as doing what is needed to reduce their sufferings, will go a long way to prevent terrorism including nuclear terrorism.

Specific Measures

(a) Strict accounting of every gram of nuclear material in accordance with full physical security standards laid down by International Atomic Energy Agency (IAEA) must be carried out by all countries and monitored under arrangements of IAEA.

(b) Nuclear power and research reactors must be made sabotage and pilferage proof. The security system should be frequently checked out through realistic exercises.

(c) The containment building housing a power reactor could be subjected to an attack similar to the one on the World Trade Centre (the 9/11 Event). Though containment domes are robust constructions, some experts apprehend that a possibility exists of "unmitigated loss of coolant" accident and significant release of radiation into the environment. To prevent this, 'no-fly' zones must be created and aggressive air defence catered for to defend these.

(d) If despite all our efforts, terrorists succeed in acquiring a nuclear bomb or material, an organization to locate and de-activate terrorist nuclear weapons needs to be created. The USA's Nuclear Emergency Search team (NEST) provides a good model.

(e) Radioactive materials used in medicine and industry, even though in small quantities, should be carefully guarded and accounted for.

(f) Nuclear weapons design must have "Permissive Action Links" (PAL)—electronic locks that must be opened for a nuclear detonation to take place. Every nuclear weapon state must have their own PAL. The bomb must have controls on its arming process and environmental sensors to prevent it from being dropped at a wrong place. From 1950 to 2000, 32 "Broken Arrow" accidents involving US/Soviet warplanes and submarines with nuclear weapons on board have taken place. Save remaining six of these 32 have been found. Without the safety devices mentioned in this sub-para, these six weapons could be misused by an enemy or a terrorist group.

Conclusion

Nuclear terrorism is not a product of science fiction. It is a reality. Every country has a responsibility to ensure that all materials are handled as per IAEA's "Action Plan for the Safety and Security of Radiation Sources". All necessary steps must be taken to prevent terrorists from gaining access to nuclear weapons sites and weapons grade materials. An agency like the USA's NEST to locate and deactivate terrorist nuclear weapons would be the last line of defence in the defence of one's own city or town from nuclear attack.

3

Intelligence Gathering in Today's World

Lt Gen Kamal Davar, PVSM, AVSM

History is replete with examples of nations and organizations largely attributing their security failures to lack of adequate, hard and timely intelligence. Whenever strategic surprise or security related lapses occur, accusations of intelligence failures are the most convenient fall-out, at times rightly, but more often than not, wrongly as a cover-up for other failings. Both Kargil and the recent Mumbai mayhem were essentially systemic shortcomings and it is grossly unfair to brand them exclusively as intelligence failures. Conversely, intelligence agencies get credit rarely for any strategic or tactical successes. For obvious reasons, details of intelligence successes must remain shrouded in secrecy. Practitioners of the craft of intelligence must remain quiet as there is no place for drum beating in the business of intelligence.

Intelligence is a vital tool in the overall security management of a nation and contributes substantially towards national policies and decision-making which may be critical to the very existence of the state. Political and economic intelligence have acquired similar strategic significance as intelligence related to security and military related matters. Intelligence indisputably is one of the ingredients of successful statecraft along with economic power, diplomacy, military capabilities, state-of-the-art technologies, etc. Notwithstanding its significance, since independence, we have given the importance it deserves or have made efforts to inject some energy into this critical capability and skill, only when we have been totally and harshly surprised.

The last 15 years especially have seen a rapidly deteriorating security environment in South Asia. Our intelligence, during this period, has been conspicuous by its absence in some of the countries in our volatile neighbourhood where anti-India plots were hatched and violence ridden actions perpetrated in the Indian hinterland with virtual immunity. The Pakistani intrusion in the Kargil Sector in May 1999 symbolized the abject failure of our intelligence machinery apart from other shortcomings in our overall security architecture. Subsequently, the frequently occurring terrorist strikes in various cities of India in the last few years culminating in the ISI executed Mumbai terrorist strike on 26 November 2008 tellingly exhibited our lack of security and intelligence preparedness. The moot question is whether intelligence agencies the world over really learn from intelligence setbacks. Most security experts feel that intelligence failures beget additional funds and additional organizations.

Defining Moments in Indian Intelligence

In the last few decades, for the Indian Intelligence, the defining moments, which stand out are firstly, the raising of the Research and Analysis Wing (R&AW) in September 1968 as an aftermath of the lessons learnt in the 1962 and '65 operations against China and Pakistan respectively for external intelligence gathering functions. In fact, after the 1962 fiasco, a review of the performance of the Intelligence Bureau led to the creation of the Directorate General of Security (DGS). Subsequently, after the 1965 War and the Mizo Revolt of 1966, the DGS was taken away from the IB and external functions were given to the R&AW which was specially thus created and the DGS placed under its control. The second most significant step in the evolution of Indian Intelligence has been a fall-out of the Kargil War in 1999 when the country was indeed surprised with the non-detection of the major Pakistani intrusion along the Line of Control and Pak troops occupying the Kargil heights in Ladakh. The Kargil crisis led to a major and much needed review of India's higher defense management and security architecture including the nuclear aspect and intelligence reforms. The Kargil Review Committee (KRC) was headed by the eminent Defence analyst K Subhramanyam and subsequently the KRC's report was vetted by the high powered Group of Ministers (GOM) constituted by the then prime minister to study its report. The government also appointed four task forces to go into various specifics of the recommendations of the KRC. The task force on

Intelligence was headed by ex R&AW chief Gary Saxena which made significant recommendations to revamp the Indian Intelligence apparatus.

The KRC pointed out, "There is no institutionalized mechanism for coordination or objective-oriented interaction between intelligence agencies and consumers at different levels. Similarly, there is no mechanism for tasking the agencies, monitoring their performance, nor is there any oversight of the overall functioning of the agencies." The KRC also opined, " The resources made available to the defence services are not commensurate with the responsibility assigned to them. There are distinct advantages in having two lines of intelligence collection and reporting with a rational division of functions, responsibilities and areas of specialization...Indian threat assessment is a single-track process dominated by R&AW... Indian intelligence structure is flawed since there is little backup or redundancy to rectify failures and shortcomings in intelligence collection and reporting..." The task force on Intelligence recommended the creation of a tri-service Defense Intelligence Agency (DIA) as the nodal agency for the analysis of all military intelligence and to synergize the functioning of and coordinate the activities of the three Service Intelligence Directorates (SIDs). Strategic intelligence assets of the Services including those for satellite imagery and Signals Intelligence were placed under the DIA. In addition, the GOM also recommended the establishment of a National Technical Facilities Organization (NTFO) to be the single window for all technical intelligence inputs to the government including in the growing areas of satellite imagery. The Cabinet Committee accepted the recommendations of GOM's on

Security (CCS) and the DIA came into existence in March 2002 with the NTFO coming into being in late 2003 taking into it some assets of R&AW's Aviation Research Centre. The previous government also established the National Security Council (NSC) and the National Security Advisory Board (NSAB) and various coordination groups for the macro-management of intelligence in a more cohesive manner. It established the Intelligence Coordination Group (ICG) for the tasking of various intelligence-gathering agencies at the apex level. The NSA chairs the ICG and has the Cabinet Secretary, the secretaries of Home, Defense, MEA and the intelligence chiefs as members of this powerful body.

Some Challenges for Indian Intelligence

India's strategic space extends from the Straits of Malacca in the East to the Gulf of Aden in the West. In addition, India's land borders exceed 15000 km which it shares with seven countries including a small segment with Afghanistan (presently this falls in the Northern Areas of PoK). India has a coastline that is 7683 km long and an exclusive economic zone of over 2 million sq km in size. With a ring of fire surrounding India and all its neighbours in varying degrees of turbulence and uneasy relationships with India including serious and unpardonable mischief making by Pakistan since years, coupled with the sieges within makes the myriad tasks for Indian Intelligence mind-boggling. Intelligence on China remains a grey area not only to us but also to the world of intelligence as well including the US. Buoyed by its growing economic clout, China has embarked on a massive modernization programme of its armed forces and importantly in cyber warfare and space weaponry also. Its massive infrastructural development in bordering Tibet calls for careful monitoring in the long term, Indian Intelligence will have to contend with the ever-growing multi-faceted Chinese economic, military and cyber threats. Pakistan, as a failing state and at war with itself, presents for the short and midterm, many intelligence headaches for India including continuing export of terrorism to India besides its continuing violent opposition of Indian interests in our neighbouring states especially in Afghanistan. Of the most critical intelligence significance to our agencies remains the status and safety of Pakistan's nuclear arsenal especially because of the rapid Talibanisation inside Pakistan. However, the list of challenges for Indian Intelligence is virtually endless but the NSC and NSA have to prioritize this ever-growing list of intelligence threats to India. Some of these will include hard actionable inputs on cross border terrorism, infiltration and exit of armed militants, details of various non-state actors fomenting terrorism from Pakistan and Bangladesh, nexus between narcotics and arms smugglers, illegal migrations, left wing extremism (LWE), separatist movements within India aided and abetted by external powers and the activities of indigenous communal elements within India besides illegal money transactions and activities of suspect NGOs. Our North East must get far more attention than before lest it degenerates into Indian version of NWFP.

Recommendations to Energise Indian Intelligence

To successfully confront the myriad security challenges which face the nation, governments and intelligence agencies need to periodically carry out in-depth reviews and modify, if required, their policies, organizational structures and procedures and continually endeavour to upgrade their HUMINT and TECHINT capabilities besides monitoring those of the adversaries and potential adversaries. The KRC, GOM and the task forces set up after the Kargil War had addressed the entire spectrum of Indian Intelligence in a very substantial manner. It is indeed gratifying to note that most of the major recommendations of the task force on Intelligence have been implemented notably the creation of the DIA and the NTFO (now rechristened as NTRO). To these organizations was also added albeit under the IB, the multi-agency centre (MAC) in 2001, to act as a nodal point for internal security intelligence gathering and analysis which reportedly has not been able to fill the bill in intelligence concerning counter-terrorism with agencies pulling in different directions. The upgradation of TECHINT capabilities across the spectrum has been underway for sometime now and encouraging. To these structures, post Kargil, after the recent Mumbai terrorist strike, the government formed by an Act the much-debated National Investigative Agency (NIA). The NIA, contrary to earlier expectations, as the nation's first statutory super agency to deal with terrorism cases, will deal with investigation and prosecution aspects only and not have any intelligence or operational responsibilities. Hence, reliance on existing mechanisms will continue. It is thus an inadequate response to fight terrorism though it may be able to prosecute those who get caught indulging in acts of terror—for it's a reactive mechanism and not a preventive one. It may be pertinent to mention here that in mid 2008, the Administrative Commission Reforms Committee had suggested that the tasks of investigation and intelligence should be incorporated in a single entity.

National Security Council Secretariat

There is a school of thought that the NSCS has far too much on its plate than required as it serves as the secretariat for a host of structures like the NSC, NSA, NSAB, SPG, NIB, ICG et al. It has evolved to be the apex collator of áll intelligence, an intelligence assessor, evaluator, coordinator, think tank, promoter of national security consciousness and an interlocutor with foreign counterpart entities apart from being a neutral and impartial monitoring agency of other intelligence outfits. In the words of ex Army Chief Gen S Roychowdhury, in the current set-up "Coordination of intelligence at national level still seems to be the Achilles heel of the system and converting the old Joint Intelligence Committee (JIC) into the secretariat of the NSC was a thoughtless act of organizational vandalism which set back the intelligence process." The Delhi based Observer Research Foundation, has also felt that the merging of the JIC into the NSCS in 1999 was a retrograde step. The NSA may consider having its own mini-secretariat so that the intelligence analyses and policy formulations are kept independent of each other.

HUMINT Capabilities

Notwithstanding revolutionary accretions in various forms of TECHINT there is no substitute for the craft of HUMINT. This is one area in which all our intelligence agencies require substantial and qualitative improvements. Our enemies have most effectively used their human resources in covert actions, covert warfare and proxy war against us since years. We need to train for and acquire this vital capability to use if required. A civilized democracy like ours can put in place the necessary checks and balances in the system. In addition, all intelligence agencies which have a strategic or tactical operational role in intelligence need to develop, nurture and effectively employ human resources for intelligence, counter-intelligence, counterterrorism and other preventive security measures. Innovative and painstaking efforts are essential to penetrate the many layers of insurgent and terrorist outfits. Intelligence agencies are not only for intelligence collection and for analyses but must have the capability for covert actions to keep the nation's enemies in check.

TECHINT Capabilities

This is an area which has stood us well over the past many years in both peace and war. However, our adversaries are more than aware of our capabilities and have been taking suitable countermeasures to thwart our advantages in this field. Terrorists are becoming hi-tech and techno-savvy by the day. Thus, it will remain an ongoing challenge for the NTRO, the satellite imaging and signals intelligence units of the DIA besides the various technical units of the R&AW and IB to remain abreast of all technological developments in this vital field including in the areas of satellite imagery, monitoring equipment, cyber warfare, communication security and digital communications. Bureaucratic sluggishness must not put back our tech preparedness. We need to take full advantages of this Information Age.

Multi-dimensional Interactions and Open Sources Intelligence (OSINT): In today's seamless and highly interactive world, much of the information which the intelligence practitioner seeks is available in the media, internet, libraries, government records, travelling journalists and the academia. By conservative estimates, OSINT caters for nearly 80 per cent of the information sought. Intelligence personnel with useful contacts earlier must continue to be utilized and not discarded. Selective outsourcing and keeping experts in diverse fields on call can prove to be cost-effective.

Reorientation

Intelligence organizations are establishments following set norms tend to get predictable and lacking in innovation and fresh ideas, not keeping pace with emerging threats. Thus these organizations must reorient themselves to take on today's non-state actors and not confine themselves to state actors only. The US with all its resources continues to be on the back foot while dealing with the al-Qaeda and the Taliban.

Linguistic Skills

An area in which most of our agencies are very weak is the inadequacy of having well trained personnel in the required numbers in various languages especially of this region. The DIA had made a modest start with the NDA to shed popular European languages in favour of languages spoken in South Asia. We need to look at this shortcoming seriously otherwise no amount of sophisticated monitoring and interception systems will suffice. A fluency and knowledge of various dialects of local languages can be of immense advantage to the personnel posted in border areas to monitor terrorist activities because terrorists generally converse in local dialects.

Avoidance of Turf Battles

Since all intelligence agencies work for the common cause namely national security, it is their religious duty to willingly share information with sister agencies and avoid turf battles which in the end are always self-defeating and damaging for the nation.

Retaining an Apolitical Orientation

It is but natural that intelligence bosses exhibit loyalty to the government of the day. However, keeping within constitutional norms and fidelity to the political leadership of the day, the ultimate loyalty of all intelligence agencies remains totally to the nation and no political pressure sway them from their professionalism and the supreme duty to the nation. The intelligence agencies should take pride in being truly apolitical.

Governmental Overseeing on Intelligence Agencies

In India, there is no governmental or parliamentary or political overseeing in the functioning of intelligence agencies as in the USA, the UK, France and other democracies. Intelligence establishments must not remain closed societies and the infusion of transparency and accountability will surely better their performance. It is time we deliberated over this aspect keeping the Indian milieu in mind.

Police Reforms and Strengthening the Grassroots

The Indian police must get back to the professionalism and standards of the erstwhile CID and sharpen its reach by penetrative intelligence measures. Vital cogs in the entire information gathering machinery and the police at the grassroots level need to be substantially energized. Major police reforms are called for across the board to make them come up to the desired standards and a systemic overhaul is essential. Police organizations in each of the states has to suitably be modernized, technologically upgraded and strengthened by themselves with better motivation, equipment, training and then networked to a national intelligence mosaic for speedy and effective response. Intelligence for the ever-growing Naxalite/ Maoist problems will only be possible with the IB and the substantial revamp of the affected state police. The Intelligence Bureau in the areas of J&K, North East, Punjab and above all, the Naxal/Maoist affected states require far greater personnel in the field than deployed now. The rural policing should have more importance. The information system needs a change from bottom to top approach and vice versa. The government should recruit personnel from local areas where hard actionable intelligence is the prime need because their contacts with the local population, familiarity with the local language and its dialects—all these factors will help them perform more efficiently, apart from training and carefully handling this eminently useful and irreplaceable human reservoir. The MHA now under a dynamic and a no-nonsense home minister have initiated many long awaited measures to streamline our internal security architecture and thus their speedy implementation will serve the nation well.

Research and Analysis Wing

Since its creation in 1968, the R&AW has come a long way. However, we need to give it a far greater covert capability and importantly the independence and initiative that any external intelligence gathering organization requires. As they endeavour to sharpen both their HUMINT and TECHINT capabilities, their staffing, recruitment and manpower problems persist and some are not too happy with the UPSC route or their own RAS cadre either. It must be remembered that this organization is not supposed to be a police organization—though some excellent police officers have served this organization—and thus it must attract the best at an early age from all the government services and also from direct recruitment from a variety of disciplines, be they scientists, economists, academicians, linguists, bankers etc.

The Defence Intelligence Agency

The DIA, raised in March 2002, got off to a flying start producing within one week of its raising, intelligence assessments despite meagre resources at its disposal as the three Services understandably took a lot of time to shed resources for the DIA. The government issued a charter with remarkable clarity after many deliberations with the three Services. The DG DIA is the Principal Military Intelligence Adviser to the Raksha Mantri, the Chairman Chiefs of Staff Committee and the defence secretary. His task is to coordinate the functioning of the three Services Intelligence Directorates, produce integrated intelligence assessments for the defence ministry and national security planners as also he controls the strategic technical assets of the Services. He also controls the functioning of our Attaches posted abroad and looks after the foreign attaches posted in Delhi. Though the DIA is doing its task well, the three Services must provide adequate and suitable work force to DIA so that it has a credible HUMINT capability also. The KRC had also opined that more than one agency must be tasked for HUMINT abroad to achieve the requisite redundancy. The DIA will only seek military information abroad and thus our civilian intelligence brethren must not feel the dilution of their responsibility. In addition, there are a large number of military or quasi-military governments in the emerging world who will liaise better with their uniformed community from the DIA. Besides, the government should change the nomenclature of DG MI's to DG Army Intelligence as the overall inter-services coordination now rests with the DIA. In addition, to ensure a better intelligence product and camaraderie between different intelligence agencies there must be far greater mutual representation in each other's entities.

A National Intelligence Authority

There is a talk that India needs a central intelligence on the lines of the US Office of the Director of National Intelligence (ODNI) who controls the entire US intelligence including the CIA, FBI, DIA, NSA and a dozen other intelligence agencies. It is felt that India too needs a central intelligence authority for collation, analysis, synthesis and dissemination for all intelligence assessments and a central coordinating body for all national intelligence. This apex body should also be responsible for long-term assessments on all aspects of national security including the nuclear, space and strategic weapons programmes of potential adversaries. It should also be the repository of the entire database on terrorist organizations and served by state of the art automation for accurate and speedy assessments for top policy and decision makers of the country. It is felt that this supreme organization will be able to synergize the entire intelligence endeavours of the nation in a more coordinated and effective manner to confront the security challenges of the future. In early 2009, the Standing Committee on Defence has advocated the need for a federal central agency that will have under its ambit all intelligence including that of the armed forces. It came down heavily on all intelligence agencies including that of the armed forces for lack of coordination and reluctance in information sharing. This aspect needs an in-depth analysis by the new government and the security community keeping in mind the Indian security environment specifically and our existing capabilities.

Conclusion

By any standards, the security environment engulfing India and the region remains volatile that calls for the security and intelligence organs of the state to remain on high alert. The recent event in Pakistan, which is in full danger of imploding, adds another alarming dimension to our security problems and consequently the major challenge for our intelligence community. After the Kargil War and now, there have been some accretions to our intelligence set-ups. As the battle against terrorism we have to gear up on our own as regards intelligence is concerned for no other country is ever going to give us any credible inputs. It will also be prudent to let our relatively new organisations mature in their mandated roles besides giving them the wherewithal to fulfill their missions as required. On vital national security issues, major political parties need to come together and unite against terror rather than demean the nation by a propensity in scoring brownie points against each other. Intelligence is the first line of defence to ensure security. It is a veritable force multiplier—a sine qua non for all the intelligence organs of India. They must shed their old baggage of carving out intelligence empires. They are to protect, the collective community skills instead, which will make India ever ready to confront any challenges it faces in its march forward.

Endnotes

1. The article is an abridged version from the Talk delivered by Lt Gen Kamal Davar at the USI on 13 May 2009.
2. Kargil Review Committee Report (15 Dec 1999), Govt of India, "From Surprise to Reckoning" extensively referred to for the above article.

4

Chinese Intelligence: Objectives and Operations

DS Rajan

Presently, the intended aim of all the institutions in the People's Republic of China (PRC) including the intelligence establishments is to serve one goal—build and protect China's peaceful development. The only difference in this regard is that the intelligence organizations enjoy the rights to conduct covert operations. It would be appropriate to start the discussion on the subject with a look at the PRC's progress so far towards achieving all-round development.

Politically, the internal situation in China largely remains stable since the introduction of reforms in 1978. The country has been free of power struggles seen in the past, with the ouster of former premier Zhao Ziyang, from his positions in the aftermath of 1989 student demonstrations, being the only exception. The authorities have been able to manage the separatist troubles in Xinjiang and Tibet as well as social problems, which have arisen out of negative aspects of reforms.

In the economic sphere, China's accomplishments are unprecedented for a developing nation. The PRC's economy has now emerged as third in the world, after that of the US and Japan. Its foreign exchange reserves – about US$ 2 trillion is the largest in the globe; its per capita GDP has grown by almost ten times to US$ 3259 as against a meager US$ 327.27 in 1991. China has become the biggest exporting nation globally, a position so far held by Germany. The PRC's requirement of raw material from abroad to speed up its development at home has grown significantly; it has emerged as the third biggest consumer of oil in the world, consuming about 16 per cent of global energy resources. Energy security has emerged as an important component of China's foreign policy. According to assessments, China's Gross National Product (GNP) could overtake that of Japan by 2010 and perhaps that of the US by 2020. Beijing has officially declared the goal of quadruplicating by 2020 the country's GDP of 2000 to attain the status of a medium level advanced nation by 2050. It also aims at completing the 'military modernization' task by middle of the century.

Externally, China has been able to exploit its economic power for expanding its political space; its influence on world events and bodies, including the UN where it is a permanent member of the Security Council, is growing fast.

China's security perceptions are undergoing a change concurrently with its ongoing development. It finds that internationally, the increasing economic interdependence and inter-connectivity have lowered the risk of worldwide large-scale wars for a relatively long period. Nevertheless, China recognizes the new challenges like struggle for strategic resources, regional conflicts, local wars, international military competition and hotting up of arms race in some regions. Regionally, it characterizes the Asia-Pacific security situation as stable, noting particularly the positive turn that has taken place across the Taiwan straits, but also acknowledges the existence of negative factors like conflicting claims over territorial and maritime rights, consolidation of regional alliances by the US and containment of China from outside and sabotage by separatist and hostile forces inside.

China has evolved a two pronged approach to sustain the prevailing favourable political, economic and security environment as mentioned above—domestically, with a new course of 'balanced development' and 'harmonious socialist society' and externally, with introduction of a 'harmonious world' concept, aiming for a win-win international situation. In particular, the PRC is paying attention to formulating suitable security and intelligence doctrines capable of guaranteeing the country's peaceful development; the focus is clearly on ensuring internal cohesion and neutralizing perceived threats from abroad to the country's sovereignty. What follows is an examination of Chinese intelligence objectives and operations in such a context.

Clandestine Procurement of Technology

The PRC needs advanced technology available abroad—banned for exports—for strengthening its modernization process. For this purpose, it depends on the services of the country's premier intelligence agency, the ministry of state security (MSS), established in 1983. The Chinese parliament, the National People's Congress, gave that year a charge to the MSS to ensure the security of the State through effective measures against enemy agents, spies, and counter-revolutionary activities designed to sabotage or overthrow China's socialist system. The MSS, besides its allotted functions abroad, is responsible for counter-intelligence work inside China, particularly against any spying activities of foreign missions, dealing with internal dissidents and monitoring domestic religious activities including those belonging to Falun Gong. It enjoys powers to arrest or detain people under Article 4 of the Criminal Procedure Law. For clandestine procurement of advanced technology, the MSS reportedly has its officers under cover in the PRC embassies abroad and runs a number of agents in foreign locations; the US alone reportedly has about 3000 agents (BBC News, Tim Luard, 22 July 2005). For the same purpose, it has set up front organizations like the Belgian-based Chinese Students and Scholars Association and front companies in Hong Kong. In this regard, the MSS is also applying pressure on immigrant Chinese community and Chinese students in the West. Among Chinese agents in the US who reportedly supplied banned technology to China in recent years are Quan Shengshu who sold rocket technology to the PRC and Dong Greg Chung of Rockwell International, California, who sold information on space shuttle programme and

Delta IV Rocket to Beijing. (US Department of Justice Press Release, 16 July 2009).

The "Second Department" of the People's Liberation Army's General Staff HQ is another agency involved in procurement of technology from abroad. Its concentration is on obtaining military-related technology available in advanced nations. Its overall task however is collection of military information and for this purpose, it deploys suitable military attaches at Chinese missions abroad, sends secret agents to foreign countries to collect military intelligence and analyses relevant open information available outside China. The department is also responsible for fusing the data collected through human, signal and imagery intelligence efforts. It sends finished intelligence products to the Central Military Commission. Its Institute of International Relations at Nanjing trains the designated military attaches. The Second Department's operations include the case of Martin Shi, a Silicon Valley businessperson, who shipped innovative night vision technology to China research centres including the Chinese military-affiliated North China Research Institute (www.frontpagemag.com, 31 March 2005).

The PRC is carrying out internet-based espionage to steal military secrets of developed nations like the US. The Second Department may be responsible for the same. China's aim is to disrupt the American military through internet hacking and electronic warfare like jamming and deceptions. An increasing number of hacker attacks on the US military targets are traceable to China. Military journals in the PRC have spoken about the necessity to get knowledge on the operational methods of the US military through electronic warfare. (www.strategy page. com, 25 November 2009).

Watching Chinese Dissidents and Pro-Democracy Elements Abroad

Monitoring the activities abroad of Chinese dissidents and pro-democracy elements, is another important task allotted to the MSS. "The 610 Office", a secret intelligence outfit, established for this purpose by the then Chinese President Jiang Zemin in all provinces, cities and towns in the country and operational since 10 June 1999, is specifically responsible for the same. Its principal target is Falun Gong, a religio-spiritual organization that had at one time good number of followers in China, even at the leadership levels. The '610' Office reportedly supervises eradication of Falun Gong in China besides being in charge of re-educating Falun Gong members. Outside China, it is conducting operations to infiltrate Falun Gong movement abroad. A defector from the PRC Embassy in Australia Chen Yonglin disclosed details on this account in June 2005.

Protecting sovereignty—Taiwan, Tibet and Xinjiang

It is not surprising that the three trouble spots of Taiwan, Tibet and Xinjiang are the MSS targets. The MSS, taking advantage of improved contacts taking place between the Mainland and Taiwan ever since the beginning of Kuomintang rule led by Ma Ying-jeou, uses Chinese visitors to Taiwan for espionage. A recent case (May 2009) involved the arrest in Taipei of Ma Zhongfei, manager of a Chinese Science and Technology company, on spying charges. The MSS is also recruiting local agents in Taiwan for getting information; a senior official of Taiwan

President's Office Wang Renbing, now under arrest, reportedly passed on secret information to the PRC.

Spying on the activities of the Dalai Lama appears to have become a priority for the MSS. Its officials posted under cover in New Delhi are presumably doing this job. In addition, Canadian researchers recently uncovered a Chinese cyber plot that hacked the sites of the Dalai Lama as well as the systems in the embassies abroad including that of India. The plot is code-named GhostNet. Reportedly, computers operate this. And, this set-up is located inside China (Online publication "Information Warfare Monitor", associated with the Munk Centre for International Studies, University of Toronto, as reported by *New York Times,* 29 March 2009.

Several instances of the MSS showing much interest to gather intelligence on the activities of the dissident Uyghur, who is abroad, are also coming to notice. According to press reports, the local authorities arrested an Uyghur activist named Babur Mehsut, based in Sweden, in June 2009 on charges of spying for Beijing.

Reports that China is hacking the US and foreign websites, mark a new trend demonstrating the aggressiveness in Beijing's intelligence collection. In September 2007, the US accused China of hacking the US defence department databases. In addition, a report made in 2009 by the US-China Economic and Security Review Commission to the US Congress, may appear significant. It has stated that the Chinese cyber spying under the auspices of the military is growing against the US and that the PRC has begun to broaden its national security concerns beyond a potential clash across Taiwan Straits and issues concerning its periphery. It has especially cited in this regard the conclusions of Northrop Grumman Corporation, a top Pentagon contractor (Jim Wolf, Reuters, 20 November 2009).

Watching Foreign Armies

The Third Department of the PLA General Staff HQ is responsible for monitoring the telecom traffic of the foreign armies and preparing necessary actionable reports. China's SIGINT network is most extensive in Asia-Pacific region. The platforms of the network are located at ground, sea and air levels, with the objective of monitoring signals from countries like Russia, Taiwan, Japan, South Korea and India. The SIGINT facility at Hainan tracks US naval activities. The Third Department also runs a foreign language institute at Luoyang, to train the cadres in collecting foreign military intelligence. The PRC's capabilities in ELINT, Satcom intercept, imagery and telemetry are also reportedly advancing.

Conclusion

In sum, China's intelligence priorities appear to be two folds: obtaining advanced technology from abroad through covert operations if necessary to reverse engineer the same for the benefit of its modernization drive and protecting the country's territorial integrity and sovereignty. The PRC's agencies concerned also seem to realize the importance of data analysis; their front think tanks (China Institute of Contemporary International Relations of the MSS and the China Institute of International Strategic Studies of the PLA Second Department) play important roles in this regard. Also, the Chinese intelligence collection methodology differs from those being adopted by other countries; the MSS and the Second Department prefer to use Chinese diplomats, students and businessmen visiting abroad for collecting technological intelligence not at one stroke but in a bit by bit manner and piece together the data to draw a final picture at a later stage. Most important is that such a style of data collection does not make the foreigners hostile to the approaching Chinese personnel.

5

Pakistan's Intelligence: Present and Future

MK Dhar, IPS (Retd)

Some sensible and humorous Pakistani friends say: every country has an army; in Pakistan, the Army has a country. In most countries, the people own everything; in Pakistan, the Army and its dreaded intelligence agency own everything. The Inter Services Intelligence (ISI) helped the Army to hijack every tool of governance, including its intelligence agencies. Presently, the United States has forced the military rulers to try a mix of democratic and military weapons against the Taliban, Al-Qaeda and several home-grown Jihadist *tanzeems*. However, the Pakistan Army and intelligence apparatus either have failed or have lost the appetite to fight the Islamist forces. The fearful civilians shiver precariously between a blundering army and the advancing Jihadists.

The armed forces have adopted a creed that it is the permanent political spine of Pakistan and its intelligence services; especially the Inter Services Intelligence (ISI) is the important stabilizing radar. The civilian government is made to dance to the tune of the army and the ISI. Though an integral part of the army establishment, the ISI, managed by the ministry of defence, is not the only intelligence agency of Pakistan.

The Major Intelligence Security Agencies of Pakistan

Federal Intelligence Agencies:

i. Intelligence Bureau

ii. Ehtasab (National Accountability) Bureau

Ministry of Defence:

i. Inter Services Intelligence (ISI)

ii. Inter Services Public Relations

Army:

i. Military Intelligence

ii. Special Services Group

iii. Surveyor General of Pakistan (Geographical Division)

Ministry of Interior

i. Federal Investigation Agency

ii. Narcotics Control Division.

Besides the Intelligence Bureau, the Ehtasab Bureau (National Accountability Bureau), Federal Investigation Agency, newly created Central Investigating Agency (CIA) and the Narcotic Control Division play important roles in domestic intelligence and security administration.

Growth of PIB

Pakistan Intelligence Bureau (PIB) is the inheritor of the Central Intelligence Bureau of British India. Its counterpart, the Intelligence Bureau of India, is the prime internal security and intelligence agency of the government of India. The Intelligence Bureau, one of the oldest security and intelligence edifices of the British Empire, had inherited the established skills and tools of the trade. Prior to 1958 military takeover, the PIB used to be answerable to the Cabinet Division of the Prime Minister's Secretariat. The PIB, like its Indian counterpart, covers activities of the political parties, activists and carries out internal security related functions, which encompass the entire panorama of the civil society and internal functioning of the *Jihadi tanzeems.* It is also responsible for counter-intelligence operations on Pakistani soil.

The Intelligence Bureau had gained prominence under Benazir Bhutto's last tenure. She used the agency and its controversial Director Masood Sharif to topple provincial governments and to carry out extensive surveillance on her political opponents and adversaries. Such blatant use of the IB to the consternation of the military and the ISI was used as one of the reasons for Benazir's dismissal in November 1996.

Organisationally, Pakistan IB follows the old British pattern, which is also the beaten path for the Indian Intelligence Bureau. It has strong presence in the provinces with units located at tehsil (revenue unit) and sub-divisional level. The IB has significant presence on the international borders with India and Afghanistan. It shares over 25 units with the ISI in Balochistan where a separatist battle is shaking Pakistan.

In certain sensitive operational areas like the Indian borders, NWFP, Northern Areas the ISI, Narcotics Bureau, MI Directorate and the Geographical Division also share joint responsibilities with the IB. In Gilgit and Baltistan areas, the IB shares its responsibility with the Special Services Group (SSG).

The Role of ISI

The other important intelligence agency of Pakistan that has gained global eminence is the Inter Services Intelligence (ISI). The Inter Services Intelligence Directorate was conceived, back in 1948, apparently as a nucleus inter-services co-ordination module and a tool to generate external intelligence, by Major General R. Cawthorne, an Australia-born British Army officer, who had opted for the Pakistan Army and served as the Deputy Chief of Staff of Pakistan Army.

Though the credit is given to Cawthorne, the inspiration had come from Britain. Pakistan army, a part of the united Indian Army, had inherited a Military Intelligence unit and did not require a special agency to coordinate different wings of the infant armed forces. Pakistan was also not positioned as a global player to take up a crash programme for creating an external intelligence agency like the MI6 and the CIA. At the initial stage of transfer of power, Britain needed the ISI as a companion agency to strengthen its own strategic perspectives in the region. They were keen to use this agency as a watchtower against Afghanistan, Russia and China. The British HQ also wanted the ISI for keeping a watch on the new corps of Pakistani Army officers.

However, after hijacking the democratic dispensation Pakistan army did not strictly follow the British blueprint.

Pakistan drifted closer to the USA, which had emerged as the greatest surviving power after the Second World War. With the initiation of the Cold War Pakistan was drawn to the US led coalition and security umbrellas floated by the anti-Soviet countries. The ISI, thereafter, leapfrogged to international arena as a partner agency of the CIA, Royal Saudi Intelligence and MI6.

Besides fulfilling its commitments to the US headed global intelligence and security tasking the ISI was extensively used as back as in 1958-60 to foment ethnic unrest in Northeast India and Kashmir. Gradually, the ISI emerged as the main 'proxy war' tool of Pakistan against India, which it fought through conventional intelligence operations, direct involvement, operations through Jihadi tanzeems patronized by the State and through third country operations. The sordid story is an integral part of Indo-Pak relations spanning 50 years of Pakistani 'proxy war' against India spanning Kashmir, Punjab, Northeast and hinterland operations.

It is necessary to understand the basic structure of the evil machine of Pakistan that had played decisive roles in collaboration with the Royal Saudi Intelligence, MI6 and the CIA in defeating the Cold War enemy of the West in the Soviet, Vietnam or Afghanistan. It also played significant roles in the rise of the Taliban, Al Qaeda and Islamist terrorism almost everywhere in the world. Footprints of the Jihadist activities anywhere in the world finally lead to the soil of Pakistan.

Following is the available list of illustrious heads of the ISI who had fashioned the characters of the army, dominated its political spectrum and carried out open and secret wars against its historical enemy India and enemies of its Western allies.

1. Brig Riazat Hussain, 1958 onwards.
2. Lt Gen Ghulam Jillani Khan, 1969 to early years of Zia-ul-Haq
3. Lt Gen Akhtar A Rahman, Zia regime till March 1987
4. Lt Gen Hamid Gul, March 1987-May 1989
5. Lt Gen Shamsur Rahman Kallue (Retd), May 1989-Aug 1990
6. Maj Gen Assad Durrani, Aug 1990-March 1992
7 Lt Gen Javed Nasir, March 1992- May 1993
8. Lt Gen Javed Ashraf Kazi, May 1993-June 1994
9. Lt Gen Nasim Raja, June 1994-1996
10. Lt Gen Ziauddin 1996, sacked by Musharraf in 1999. He was denied retirement benefits.
11. Lt Gen Mahmood Ahmad dismissed by Musharraf under American pressure for complicity with the 9/11 conspirators. India, it is reported, had supplied supporting material to the USA.
12. Lt Gen Ehsan-ul-Haq, posted on Oct 8, 2001. He was the Corps Commander at Peshawar. He was formerly posted at Pakistan High Commission in Delhi in the rank of Counsellor. Removed in October 2004.
13. Lt Gen Ashfaq Kiyani, appointed on Oct 4, 2004, present Army Chief
14. Lt Gen Nadeem Taj, appointed on Sept 20, 2007
15. Lt Gen Ahmad Shuja Pasha, appointed, on September 29, 2008

Functional Structure

Following are the broad divisions of the functional structure of the ISI:

1. Joint Counter-Intelligence Bureau (JCIB): It is responsible for counter-intelligence activities and operations;
2. Joint Intelligence Signal Bureau (JISB): It generates and denies Signal intelligence and liaises with the Signal Corps of the Armed Forces and the US and UK signal intelligence community;
3. Joint Intelligence Bureau (JIB): It handles political matters. One section is assigned to study and assess Indian political developments;
4. Joint Intelligence Finance (JIF): It manages budgetary and non-budgetary funds of the ISI; evaluates and approves critical operations;
5. Joint Intelligence Technical (JIT): It is responsible for technical, including EIInt, PhotoInt, ImageInt, SatInt, etc;
6. Joint Arms Direction Group (JADG): This wing is responsible for planning coordination in military exercises and procurement of weapons from unconventional sources, besides periodical evaluation of joint exercises;
7. Joint Intelligence Miscellaneous (JIM): It oversees forward intelligence tasks, sabotage and subversion operations in foreign countries. Three sections are devoted to India;
8. Joint Intelligence North (JIN): It is the hub of operations in Kashmir and other "special operations";
9. Foreign Liaison Section (FLS): Responsible for liaison with friendly foreign intelligence services;
10. Inter Services Federal Intelligence (ISFI): It supplements the intelligence efforts of the provincial

governments and often works as the direct arm of the political/military bosses in internal political matters;

11. Public and Service Groups (P&SG): It functions in close liaison with the Joint Chiefs of Staff Committee and maintains media liaison. The post-holder is generally close to Chief of the Army Staff and the top executive. The position holder is handpicked;
12. Joint Intelligence X: Its exact functional charter is not known. It is said that this wing is responsible for Intelligence estimate, threat assessment and formulation of highly Sensitive Operations, including assassination, in collaboration with the JIB, JIM, JIN and ISFI.

Operational Structure

Like most other intelligence organisations, the ISI has put in position a well-defined functional and operational structure as follows:

Director General Intelligence (DG ISI)

↓

(Three star General)

↓

Deputy Director General—Political

(Two star officer)

↓

Deputy Director General—External I

(Two star officer)

↓

Deputy Director General—External II

(Two star officer)

The number of two star officers has proliferated over years and it is estimated that four such officers of the rank of Major General (one each from the Air Force and Navy) have been put in charge of designated divisions. These are reported to be post-Nawaz Sharif developments.

The DDG (Pol) controls the territorial and subject desks and sections, which cover the activities of the political parties, student, labour, mujahideen organisations, madrassas and religious institutions, tribal affairs, internal surveillance/security duties, VIP security duties, minority affairs and anti-terrorism activities. An officer of the rank of Brigadier generally heads each sub-division. However, officers of the rank of Colonels and Majors head some of the lesser units.

The DDG-Pol continues to function with full blessings of the military dictator and is said to have been tasked to screen the election aspirants, candidates, eliminate the undesirable aspirants either by persuasion or by force and to ensure that the election returns a rubber stamp National Assembly.

The office of the DDG-External I requires some special mention. It controls the 'foreign operations' of the ISI and presides over the most dreaded wing of the ISI-counter Intelligence. It also covers the territorial, geopolitical, economic, strategic intelligence affairs in the Middle East, Africa and other countries. The DDG-Ex I also maintains liaison with the PMO (whenever there is one), and with the office of the CMLA/CEO/President, whatever designation a military dictator prefers to decorate himself with. DDG-External I is a powerful position.

DDG-External II has the onerous responsibility for coordinating activities of Joint Intelligence M and N, which are India and Kashmir specific. It also supervises and coordinates activities of the Jihadi tanzeems, which do not cross the limit imposed by the Pakistani rulers and draw attention of the US agencies. This branch also supervises the operations in Pakistan Occupied Kashmir and the Gilgit and Northern Areas.

The Rise of Jihadi

With the Al-Qaeda and Taliban establishing firm foothold on the NWFP, South and North Waziristan and Chitral Tract, the ISI is called upon to generate intelligence and assist the Army, which is fighting a losing battle in the tribal areas. It has been alleged by US observers that considerable number of rogue and Islamicised ISI and Army personnel were encouraging the Taliban and Al Qaeda forces to establish stranglehold in the tribal and frontier areas. The ISI and the Army had brokered a temporary peace with Al Qaeda and the Taliban in South Waziristan in February 2007 and later in February 2009 conceding Sharia rule to the Taliban dominated areas. The Taliban and its Al Qaeda mentors rule over the FATA and parts of NWFP. The ISI has failed to break the logjam and the army has shown reluctance to fight the tribal Talibans.

Under these circumstances Pakistani observers have commented that the Al Qaeda and Taliban are happily cohabiting with home-grown Jihadists in the interiors of Pakistan's mainland and even in cities like Lahore, Karachi and Islamabad. The ISI, IB and the Army were reluctant to confront them as the lessons of the Lal Masjid incident and loss of over 1500 soldiers in the tribal areas have scared them. There has been huge desertion from the Pakistan Frontier Guards.

However, the situation has changed since mid 2009. The Tehrik-e-Taliban, Pakistan, Al Qaeda had succeeded in forming International Jihad Front with Afghan Talibans, Jaish-e-Mohammad, Lashkar-e-Jhangvi and Huji Pakistan. After this grouping was formed the ISI got involved with Markaz-ud-Dawa and Lashkar-e-Taiba and supported them to carry out spectacular sea-borne attack on Mumbai on 26 November 2008. Since then Harkat-ul-Mujahideen and LeT continue to be main allies of the ISI. However, it must not be assumed that the ISI has no window open to Taliban and Al Qaeda. The US experts opine that the ISI is still protecting the Talibans and Al Qaeda though they are carrying out war against Tehrik-e-Taliban groups in Swat and Waziristan. This action is prompted by the US and it is known that US personnel are also fighting alongside the Pakistani forces. The hardcore enemies of the ISI amongst the Jihadists have started retaliating by regular attacks on government targets including offices of the ISI.

Though internal situation in Pakistan is not stable and there are signs of Talibanisation of the country, the ISI continue to chalk out plans to stage more spectacular attacks on India. Recent arrests of David Coleman Hadley and Rana in the USA has proved that these LeT elements were planning attack on the NDA and probably on some atomic installations.

Future Scenario

The often asked question about the future of Pakistan's Intelligence agencies cannot be answered astrologically. Evolution and reconditioning of these tools of governance would depend on the immediate future political evolution of Pakistan and its geostrategic juxtaposition alongside its allies like the USA, Saudi Arabia, and UK.

Internally, the Pakistani society is vertically and horizontally divided into three distinct camps:

(a) those aspire and want to achieve true democracy;

(b) the fundamentalist and Jihadist forces who want Taliban type regime in Pakistan and

(c) strong segments of the armed forces which want continued military hegemony.

The Talibanis and other Jihadists want to occupy the country and establish the Islamic Emirate of Pakistan alongside the Islamic Emirate of Afghanistan. The US agencies have confirmed that the ISI is in cahoots with the Afghan Taliban and they along with a section of the army would not mind reasserting their hegemony for establishing a true Islamic nation.

In this scenario, the ISI and the IB are likely to cut out fine furrows of their own between the hazardous territories dominated by International Islamic Jihadists, the ambitious leaders of the armed forces and the helpless civil society. These agencies would like to cater to all palates as far as practicable, thus preserving their own identity and interests and swinging along with the wind whichever is stronger.

Ambivalent attitude of the ISI and the Army are likely to strengthen the Jihadi bases and widen their sphere of activities in Afghanistan, Iran, Iraq, and Central Asian countries, India and Bangladesh etc, besides other theatres in West Asia, Africa, Europe and the Americas. Pakistan has become the strongest base of the Islamic Jihadist forces.

Therefore, it would be premature to assume that the Pakistani Intelligence Agencies would disarm themselves and willingly function as appendages to the civilian government. The ISI, MI and the IB are expected to support the Jihadists and political hegemony of the army. They would, in all probability, continue to escalate Jihadist activities inside India. This is further strengthened by US disclosure that the ISI had secretly brought Mullah Omar to a safe house in Karachi, where he formed a new Shura. In case Pakistan is Talibanised India may face greater danger from the ISI controlled by the Jihadists. New information reveals that the CIA is funding the ISI heavily hoping that the rogue agency would collaborate with it and fight the Jihadist forces. The future of ISI-CIA relationship cannot be predicted just now. In case Obama administration opts to root in Afghanistan and continue to fight the Pakistani Jihadists than Pakistan army and the ISI would remain in US orbit. In case US and NATO withdraw from Afghanistan and abandon the war against terrorists the Pakistan army and the ISI are sure to assume more power and pose greater threat to India.

6

Intelligence and Terrorism

Dr NC Asthana, IPS

Unrealistic Expectations from Intelligence

For the media, the politicians and the people alike, the most fashionable thing these days is to blame everything on 'intelligence failure'. By and large, the common man, the media and even the system expects that intelligence must know every stage of terrorism—who is doing talent-spotting and where; who is subverting whom and where; where the terrorists are 'merging' with the local population; who is smuggling arms, ammunition and explosives in this vast country of nearly 15,000 km land borders and 7,200 km of coastline; what are the early signs of terrorist preparations (whatever that means in official gobbledygook); where are those five terrorists in a country of over a billion, what they are thinking; where are they going to explode the next bombs; would the target include sensitive and vital establishments, religious places, places of public importance and the economic infrastructure; which political personality they are going to assassinate and how; which religious gathering they are going to attack so as to precipitate communal tension; and which five-star hotel or IT company they are going to hit next, to name a few.

Not only that, the media expects the intelligence to penetrate the minds of every citizen in this vast country of over a billion and to listen to everything that is being talked about in this massive country. They want the intelligence to know what some people might have talked in utter secrecy. How in the world would they be able to do so, is never spoken of. Everybody thinks that they are 'secret' people; and in that case, they should have some 'secret' ways—they should be able to get their things and do their work secretly.

If there was an Advance Warning, Nothing should have happened

Every terrorist strike leads to a bout of accusations and counter-accusations between the actors involved. The intelligence community says that it had warned the police. The police say that the warning was not actionable. The media says that the intelligence should have known all that was about to happen, and the police should have been able to prevent all of them. In this game of universal ignorance, nobody understands that even if an intelligence warning had been issued that there was likelihood of a terrorist strike in a city by a certain group; the fact is that there is pretty little that can be done to prevent it. Can the police arrest all those 'hidden agents' of the said terrorist group in a large city or for that matter even in a small city? It is not possible because, by their very nature, the so-called hidden agents of the terrorist group are not identified. Had they been known, the police would have them rounded up much earlier even without the intelligence input! Further, can the police afford to protect the thousands of potential targets in a metropolis? Is it possible to keep everything in a metropolis under observation or under secret cameras? It is only for places like a cinema hall where bags can be banned—not in a market! In a country like India we have an average of 122 policemen for one hundred thousand people, what exactly they can do and what exactly they are supposed to do and which they do not do to incur blame? Even if all sorts of leave are cancelled and put every single policeman from the constable to the chief of the state police on the roads, there will still be millions of places which will not be covered by them.

Espionage or Human Intelligence and its limitations

Espionage centres on recruiting and handling human sources (agents) to acquire "protected" or "denied" information. Espionage done by professionals is more drudgery than glamorous and there are, in real life, but few agents who bear any resemblance to these fictional spies compounded of chilled steel and intrigue.

Admittedly, espionage is the most difficult intelligence discipline to conduct. You simply cannot place an agent anywhere at will. Cultivation, recruitment and infiltration all take considerable time and demand great skill in inter-personal relationships, persuasion, human psychology and knowledge of the agent's social environment on the part of the handler.

Motivating and Causal Factors in becoming an Informer or Agent

In the modern context, the following types of men are likely to become agents or sources:

a) One who is seeking rewards of some kind. These rewards could be in the form of money, sex, a particular lifestyle that would have been normally beyond his means, travel abroad, facility of studying abroad for his children or anything that he had been secretly craving for in his life and has not been able to get.

b) One who is ideologically committed against the target.

c) One who has some sort of racial, cultural, religious or linguistic affinity with a 'foreign' country or organization; or he could have marital relations in that country or have some relatives there.

d) One who is a secret admirer of a 'foreign' country or organization and, at the same time, considers himself to be a misfit in his own country or organization for whatever reason. The latter belief could eventually make him feel alienated or suffer from an isolationist mind-set.

e) One who is prone to blackmail on account of anything—that could be his shady past; any misdeeds that he has so far kept carefully buried; his perverse sexuality; his abuse of drugs or alcohol; or any aspect of his life that he does not want to be exposed; say, for example, his extramarital escapades.

f) One who is disgruntled or is seeking revenge on account of any persecution that he might have suffered at the hands of the State or his organization; gross social or political injustice meted out to him; having been victim of some riot or atrocities at the hands of security forces either himself or his family members/relatives; or merely an obsessive feeling that the State had been discriminating against his community.

g) One who is seeking some thrill or adventure in life.

h) Mixed motives involving two or more of the above.

The relative importance of these motivations and causal factors varies greatly. It depends on the person as well as on his environment.

Vulnerable Personality Profiles

The concept central to the whole phenomenon of espionage is that of "betrayal of trust." A spy betrays the trust which his organization or country had reposed in him. A truly conscious source is one who is betraying, knowing fully well what he is doing, and only he qualifies to be called a spy, agent, or source. Those who are not conscious of their act of betrayal are merely "sources of information"; to call them spies, agents or sources is professionally incorrect.

Why is it difficult to raise 'Informers' in Terrorist Organizations?

Indian media, people and even intelligence officers have not been able to understand that there are intrinsic limits within which the motivating/ causal factors of financial temptation; ideology; racial, cultural, religious or linguistic affinity; blackmail; or desire to take revenge can be exploited.

There is no way one can exploit the factors of racial, cultural, religious or linguistic affinity with terrorists simply because it does not exist at all in such situations—many of them come from the same society. Many of the factors that could be profitably used in some other situation cannot be used with a terrorist. You cannot blackmail a terrorist because he is already on the wrong side of the law and does not bother about what society would think of him. As far as the desire to take revenge against some sort of injustice or persecution is concerned, it could, in fact, be one of the things that made him a terrorist in the first place! That leaves ideology, which is even more useless in such a situation—he is already ideologically committed. One cannot reasonably think of a situation where a man might have risen to the core group of a terrorist organization and yet he would secretly hate its ideology to such an extent that he would betray it.

Then there is a serious problem with penetrating the core. Penetrating the core is quite a daunting task. The core is usually very small, say four or five members and the information pertaining to crucial decisions is limited to them only. Even if one of them is subverted somehow the source cannot go on reporting indefinitely. Core groups are generally small. An isolated leak could be attributed to a multitude of possible origins. However, a succession of leaks would invariably arouse suspicion. Then, by using a process of successive elimination of various possibilities, loyal members can locate the source of the leak. He would be killed in no time, and the operation would come to an end.

Then there are other problems related to penetration. The Kashmiris, for example, are so fair-skinned and have such distinctive features that it is very difficult for a relatively dark-skinned intelligence operative from any other part of India say Bihar or Tamil Nadu to infiltrate a terrorist organization in Kashmir even if he is a Muslim and knows Islamic practices better than anyone of the terrorists. The same problem arises when they have to penetrate an organization in the northeastern parts of India where most people have Mongoloid features.

Then comes the question of inducement. The media does not understand that not everybody can be purchased with money. The terrorists are materially different from ordinary criminals. They are not there for making money or for enjoying a lifestyle which the gang leaders in movies based on the lives of Mafiosi have. Most of them are fanatically committed people and cannot be bought with money.

It is only the fringe which lacks commitment and which may be bought with money—not the core. Had they not been committed they could not have reached that position in the first place. The fringe does not have access to crucial information. Hence even if you subvert a fringe member with money and even if he gives you some information, it will be superficial information only—the maximum to which he has access. The information given by such fringe sources, for their own survival, should be such that it could theoretically be in the possession of many people and also not very sensitive, making it difficult to trace the source of the leak.

The Myth of the Panacea of Technical Intelligence

Technical intelligence is popularly believed to be the panacea of all the weaknesses of intelligence. The myth is that by some secret method, the intelligence agencies should be able to get all the information about terrorists without taking the trouble of making any source and without touching anybody. People think that these days some mysterious bugs have been invented and if our intelligence agencies are not using them, they must be fools!

For their information, there are serious practical problems in using bugs in remote or rural areas. Bugs, however, sophisticated they be, have their own technical limitations, mostly related to range of transmission and power supply. Theoretically, it is possible to solve those problems but in practice it may often not be cost-effective or practicable. The bugs can be used effectively only in certain situations. For example, if a visiting foreign dignitary is staying in a hotel, it is very easy to bug the room and park a car in the parking lot of the hotel where the transmission would be picked up. Now consider a madrasa in a remote rural area, say, near the Indo-Nepal border. A bug planted there would be starved of power and where can you pick up the signal? And finally, who has decreed that the target people are obliged to talk only inside that madrasa building and not elsewhere? They could talk and conspire anywhere—in any house, any field, anywhere! All your bugs would remain in place and yet would not be able to do anything.

Conclusion

There are intrinsic limitations in the entire business of intelligence about terrorism. Nations that refuse to accept them will be guilty of misleading their people in the fight against terrorism.

7

Asymmetric Warfare

Lt Gen PC Katoch, UYSM, AVSM, SC, (Retd)

Asymmetric wars have no rules, no regulations and no boundaries. Their aim is to take advantage of the weaknesses of the adversaries while maximizing their own strength, achieving disproportionate effect. Today's conflict situations show the most effective response from a state against superior operational power of an opponent is crafty diplomacy, wily espionage, terrorism (including cyber terrorism), low intensity conflict or proxy war, employment of weapons of mass destruction like dirty/ chemical/radiological bombs through non-state actors and a host of other asymmetric approaches. The principles of asymmetric war are not to use armed forces to compel the enemy to submit to one's will but use all means including armed forces, military and non-military, lethal and non-lethal measures to compel the enemy to accept one's interests.

There are many definitions of asymmetric warfare. The US military states that adversaries are likely to attempt to circumvent or undermine US strengths while exploiting its weaknesses, using methods that differ significantly from the usual mode of US operations... asymmetric warfare consists of unanticipated or non-traditional approaches to circumvent or undermine an adversary's strength while exploiting his vulnerabilities through unexpected technologies or innovative means.

The 9/11 was a benchmark on the global geostrategic plane. This cataclysmic event ushered in a totally new security paradigm causing a realignment of old and existing alliances. The US mainland was hit for the first time since its independence and US public came face to face with an enemy that had no face, no identity and yet could strike deep in its territory and seemingly go unchallenged. Erstwhile US perception of West Asia as the breeding ground for terror, in consonance with world opinion, veered towards Sudan, Iraq, Afghanistan and Pakistan. Although a very aggressive policy has been followed against the first three, Pakistan has been meted a soft approach owing to her geostrategic location and continued US presence in Afghanistan.

The 9/11 and its aftermath made the US realize its vulnerabilities and sensitized it to the issue of terrorism, which India has been suffering for decades. Although US has dithered from extending the war on terrorism into Pakistan, other than Predator UAV strikes, despite reports of presence of al-Qaeda and Taliban leadership in

Pakistan, US does publicly acknowledge the need for Pakistan to act firmly against terrorists within Pakistan. This 'soft US approach' is in their national interest albeit US recognize India as a key partner in the global coalition against terrorism and is in the process of enlarging a strategic partnership with us. The US policy towards Pakistan aims at addressing concerns like national/global security, nuclear proliferation, economic and strategic opportunities in South Asia, democracy, and anti-Americanism in the Muslim world. She also wants Pakistan to tread the path of a true democracy to become a stable and responsible member of the international community, at peace with its neighbours.

As India aspires to be a regional power with global aspirations, there is a need to identify and monitor asymmetries vis-à-vis our opponents and develop responses. Increased attention to asymmetric warfare is only justified and timely. Asymmetric war is waged against a nation and not against the military alone. There is no domain that asymmetric warfare cannot use, and there is almost no domain, which does not have war's offensive pattern. It can be waged on numerous planes and has many forms like diplomatic, financial, unconventional, proxy war/low intensity conflict, terrorism, fourth generation war, networks, biochemical, NBC, intelligence, resources, ecological, psychological, economic, space, energy, regulatory, electronic, drugs/smuggling, sanctions, media, virtual, ideological, etc.

Asymmetric wars exploit the fault-lines of the adversary, instigating weaker/underprivileged sections of the society, propagating to its advantage the issue of poor political health of a nation, exploitation of the diversity based on caste, creed, and community and expressing ethnic affinity towards a particular segment of masses to arouse anti-government sentiments etc. Such methods adopted to target different sections of the society lead to waging asymmetric war on different planes. It goes without saying that our adversaries will relentlessly seek ways to block India's rising power through asymmetric warfare.

Asymmetric warfare could be transnational, related to international terror networks such as al-Qaeda and Lashkar-e-Taiba or sub-national like Maoists/Naxalites/ULFA and other ethnic separatist groups. Asymmetric fighters may or may not wear uniforms, or even share a common language, but they are defined by their stated objectives. There is no distinction between frontline and hinterland and between combatants and non-combatants. Such war could be fought on ethnic, religious and ideological grounds with psychological will of the adversary as the target. Attacks on our Parliament, J&K Assembly, Kaluchak, Tanda, Akshardham, Ayodhya and 26/11 are all examples. The focus is to collapse the target states internally or political functioning morally and to rob its will to continue with the conflict. The emphasis is on destroying the will of the enemy. The asymmetric warrior is educated, techno-savvy, can exploit cyber space and merge in an urban milieu. Globalization has helped him by providing better communications, easy travel and quick transfer of money digitally or through Hawala/narco transactions. Asymmetry through non-war operation encompasses fields like finance, ecology, psychology, media, drug trafficking tech etc. These asymmetric approaches will invariably be used in conjunction with others.

Asymmetric forces are usually lightly equipped with small arms, mines, improvised explosive devices and rocket propelled grenades. Tactical and strategic levels merge as the targets encompass military, political and civil entities. Terrain is used as a force multiplier and population is used for providing supplies and vital intelligence. Logic bombs, computer viruses and network disruptions are also used to cause fear and disrupt command and control networks. Their operations multiply fear in the civil population gaining control over the masses. If this fear is allayed their effectiveness would significantly degrade. Psychological operations, therefore, become the dominant operation and strategic weapon.

A recent addition to asymmetric warfare has been fourth generation war, already being enacted in Iraq and Afghanistan. Fourth generation war is based on the premise that superior will can defeat a greater economic and military power if employed properly. Aim is to convince the adversary that his strategic goals are unachievable or too costly for perceived benefits. It focuses on changing minds of decision makers by using media supplemented with internet as the primary avenue for moulding opinion. Material easily available in society like fertilizer, gasoline etc is used. A dissension base is essential, which can be ignited with idea and money both of which are digitally transferable.

Pakistan chose to wage asymmetric war against India decades ago. Our failure to recognize this as an "asymmetry" and respond commensurately has encouraged Pakistan to continue with her policy of "a thousand cuts" and a deniable stance. The two-nation theory is not the driving force behind this Pakistani stance. It is more to do with her complex ridden mindset that is marked by permanent hostility towards India and a compulsive urge to take advantage of every difficulty faced by India along with a burning desire to prevent the emergence of India as a major regional or global power. While we keep extending a hand of friendship to Pakistan, we fail to understand that in asymmetric warfare, all friendships are influx, with self-interest the only constant and that in Pakistan's perception her self-interest is a weak, balkanized India. Added to this is her feeling of having acquired a psychologically asymmetric advantage over India due to her nuclear capability. Faced off with state sponsored/non-state actors, India recognized international rules of engagement for resolving differences is outplayed and at a distinct disadvantage.

Pakistan's inadequate economy constrains her from matching India. She will continue her nuclear blackmail bogey to make the world pay a ransom. Kashmir would remain centric to her interests and her so-called 'freedom fighters' would continue to bleed India. Concurrently, Pakistan would lean on China to assist modernize her military. This would also be to China's advantage. Peace with India will result in calls for greater democracy in Pakistan, which is unlikely to be acceptable to the Pakistan Army. Over a thousand serving and retired officers from Pakistan's armed forces have been infiltrated into every level of bureaucratic and financial control in that country; inducted at senior levels in the federal, provincial, government and semi-government departments – entrenched into money making despite hefty pay packets. There is little chance that the Pakistan Army will let go of this power and money. Confrontation with India is, therefore, likely to continue unabated as peace with India will make the Pakistani populace demand the armed forces return to the barracks and forgo their hold in the federal, provincial, government and semi-government departments.

China unambiguously wants to rein supreme not only in Asia but in the world. Having studied the Gulf, Afghanistan and Iraq wars, China is evolving a strategy to fight the US without fighting a war. This would be largely through application of deniable asymmetric approaches, making full use of revolution in military affairs including Net-centric and information warfare. Some of these measures would be used against India as well. Economic war with China is predictable from the near to long term future. China will attempt to inflict economic damage rather than military damage (though skirmishes/ conflicts and incursions cannot be ruled out) directed towards enforcing embargo on Indian sea borne trade with the two fold aim of signalling her supremacy in Asia Pacific region and edge out and constrain India and other ASEAN nations, thereby signalling to the USA that the world is back to bi-polarity.

Potential asymmetric threats could be in the spheres of weapons of mass destruction coupled with information operations, non-war operations. A nuke or a dirty bomb could be brought in by a hundred methods, and positioned against a countervalue target by competent special forces led terrorists. Of course, the "threat" of using nukes directly against India itself is a powerful asymmetric measure at the strategic level. A nuke can pose the greatest asymmetric threat when used in a tech non-lethal mode as the generator of high altitude electromagnetic pulse that will threaten the information systems. The US is desperate for a national missile defence to shield it from a high altitude electromagnetic pulse attack. At 300 kilometres, a burst centred over Nebraska could generate high altitude electromagnetic pulse over ninety per cent of USA. A high altitude electromagnetic pulse attack simply destroys every electronic chip.

Additionally, Pakistan and China are both suspect of maintaining chemical weapons and are believed to have productionised operational quantities of biological weapons as well. Chemical weapons have a track record of use through the last century, which probably implies they will continue to be employed. Number of delivery options including special forces and non-state actors exist. It would be difficult to trace the origin. Their application against non-combatant population could be an attractive option that would stress Indian capabilities and cloud the battlefield. A biological attack may not even be cognizable for long after its launch.

How should India respond? A conventional response is ineffective in face of asymmetric threats. Asymmetric approaches can achieve powerful effect through manipulation of the psychological element. Aimed directly at the will of the opponent, they can compensate for material or other deficiencies. While the method of approach may be tactical, the psychological effect is sought at the strategic level. This is the characteristic of asymmetry;

the continuous focus on strategic effect, enabled by reliance on the psychological component of the approach selected. In functional terms the mind of the opponent is the target which should be exploited. Effective asymmetric operations cause a disproportionate amount of damage to the target nation for the investment in resources, time and money by the attacker. Hence, it is important that the fault lines of Pakistan and China be identified and used to our advantage. This alone would be an effective deterrent to stop Pakistani and Chinese asymmetric approaches.

In addition to the above, a proactive strategy needs to be put in place to 'deny a potential adversary from exploiting our own fault lines'. Such a strategy must encompass the larger political process. This should essentially include measures like transparent, just and honest governance, provision of justice for victims of communal violence and deterrence measures against future occurrences, establishment of an effective good grievance detection, monitoring and redressal machinery, prompt relief in natural disasters, equitable economic development of backward areas and more investments in education to empower the youth to stand on their own feet, making primary education mandatory and free for all and the like. Since the asymmetric warrior draws his moral and material support from the population, isolating this support would cut off his ability to camouflage and sustain.

Focused psychological operations and genuine people oriented schemes must be systematically executed to remove causes for disillusionment and build bonds. A twin path of negotiation and hard response should be followed to target the terrorist leadership. Diplomatic efforts should be heightened not only in getting terror organizations blacklisted but also in getting their leaders isolated and declared terrorists. There is a need to profile these leaders, understand how they think, operate and inspire and what is important to them. Thereafter, their credibility should be diminished by highlighting their vulnerabilities in the media. There is a need to synchronize global political, intelligence, military, cyber and diplomatic efforts towards identifying, isolating and stemming the specific sources of financial and armed support. A concerted international focus should be directed towards tackling narco-terrorism linkages as well.

Asymmetric threats can manifest against us targeting the entire political, social, military and financial fabric of the country. Targets could be anything: nuclear facilities, dignitaries, mass transit system, harbours, hydrocarbon fuel assets, military installations, institutions, religious places, demographic invasion, financial institutions, support to terror groups through electronic warfare, cyber war, drugs, fake currency and the like. In order to emerge as a leading nation of the 21st century, India would have to develop requisite responses including in the sphere of asymmetric warfare. India's military strategy will have to be effective across the entire spectrum of possible conflicts – from a high intensity conventional war under the backdrop of a nuclear, biological and chemical threat to low intensity conflict which may include high intensity insurgency, militancy and terrorism.

There is a very clear requirement to focus attention on the conflict spectrum below the threshold of war, particularly asymmetric threats. Response to an asymmetric threat has two facets, viz. defensive and offensive. Defensive measures imply identifying the threat and taking proactive measures to negate the same so that the adversary is not able to exploit them but the most effective method of fighting asymmetric war is to initiate a step by step offensive approach; to ensure effective placement of measures in advance that can be activated when considered necessary. The instruments of response available are diplomacy, intelligence agencies, law enforcement organizations, conventional and special forces. Special forces are being employed world over to optimize the efficacy of the interests of state power as well as deterrence. More importantly, deterrence is effective only if the capability is demonstrated. The fields available for forging asymmetric war on the adversary are diplomatic warfare, financial warfare, resource warfare, electronic warfare including cyber war, guerilla warfare, ideological warfare, fourth generation war and the like.

The idea that state or non-state actors will attempt to find innovative ways to exploit our weakness is the basis for asymmetry. The target for all asymmetric approaches is the will of the opponent and this is achieved through the pursuit of psychological effects at the strategic level, regardless of the level of war on which the asymmetric approach is employed. A dynamic process of threat and responses is an inescapable factor in any analysis of asymmetry. Disparity of interest is a key factor in assessing an adversary's incentive to adopt asymmetric approaches. We should be clear that a number of opponents are exploring and employing strategies to keep India from growing. This is a "dirty war" which needs to be responded in equal measure.

8

The Menace of Terrorism

Lt Gen SK Sinha, PVSM (Retd)

The biggest menace facing humankind today is terrorism. Millions of innocent lives have been lost due to terrorism in the last half a century. However, terrorism per se is not a new phenomenon in history. The acts of terrorism have been taking place through the ages. The massacres by Chengiz Khan, Timur or Nadir Shah were acts of State terrorism. So were in recent times, the Cultural Revolution in China and the genocide by the Pol Pot regime in Cambodia. In the past, strong perpetrated terrorism against the weak. Lately, the world has been witnessing terrorism of the weak against the strong. The 9/11 is a classic example. Terrorist groups have been causing large-scale casualties of innocent citizens to achieve their nefarious designs. They have unleashed a virtual war against the State and the society.

The UN Security Council has defined terrorism as an act intended to cause death of civilians or non-combatants with a view to intimidate the government or the society in pursuit of political, ideological or religious goals. The latter is often referred to as Jehadi terrorism. Brigadier SK Malik of the Pakistan Army, a favourite of General Zia-ul-Haq known as the Mulla in Khaki, has written a book on the Quranic concept of warfare. He maintains that the human race is a bifocal society comprising believers and non-believers. The believers must be constantly at war with the non-believers until they are killed or they are converted to Islam. Striking terror amongst the non-believers must be the constant aim. It is not a means to an end but an end in itself. Through striking terror, the non-believer should lose faith in him, in his religion, in his polity and in his State. The infamous al-Qaeda has a similar philosophy. It aims to establish a Caliphate, where Nizam-e-Mustafa will prevail. The world is divided into Dar-ul-Islam and Dar-ul-Harb. In the former, Islam prevails and in the latter, other religions are dominant. Dar-ul-Harb has to embrace Dar-ul-Islam.

There are three types of terrorisms: secessionist, revolutionary and religious or Jehadi terrorism. India has been a victim of all these types of terrorism. We have suffered terrorist depredations for much longer than any other country in the world. We have faced secessionist terrorism in the North East, revolutionary terrorism of Naxals and both variations of Jehadi terrorism, one in which people's support is available and the other in which it is not. Jehadi terrorism in Kashmir has the support of a sizeable section of the local people. We have also been facing the other version of Jehadi terrorism with virtually no popular support. The repeated terrorist attacks in many of our mainland cities fall in this category. Among these, the 26/11 Mumbai attack was in a class of its own. It was a terror war unleashed by Pakistan against India.

The terrorist is normally an invisible enemy. His strongest weapon is surprise, compounded by his commitment to sacrifice his life. The Jehadi terrorist is thoroughly indoctrinated. He is ever willing to undertake suicide missions. He is convinced that if he sacrifices his life for the holy cause, the gates of heaven and eternal bliss will open for him. When the terrorist gets deluded to believe that he can successfully fight a conventional battle against regular forces, he is destined to fail. The LTTE in Sri Lanka was the most well-organized terrorist organization of the world. It had pioneered the concept of suicide attacks. It had naval and air wings and it made good use of them. A worldwide network was available to it, ensuring free flow of funds and weapons. It had a very powerful leader who commanded unquestioned loyalty from its cadres. It overestimated its strength and decided to fight a conventional final battle with Sri Lanka's regular forces. In the process, it was wiped out.

We need to put our record of dealing with terrorism under the scanner to draw appropriate lessons. While doing so, I shall draw on my experience as Governor of Assam for six years and thereafter of Jammu and Kashmir for five years. Let me first emphasize that no war is won by fighting only defensive action. Wars are won through offensive action. Dealing with terrorism through defensive measures alone, cannot eliminate this menace. Matters are further complicated if there are serious flaws in the defensive measures that are dispersion of resources in trying to defend too many likely terrorist targets. This only weakens our ability to deal with the terrorist menace. The Napoleonic maxim that he who tries to be strong everywhere ends up being strong nowhere, is equally true in the war against terror. In the ultimate analysis, success is achieved by destroying the terrorist's capability to attack.

Cross-border terrorism started in Kashmir in 1989 and cross-border illegal migration in Assam started much earlier. The latter led to insurgency erupting in that State in 1979. Our reaction to the former has been purely defensive and to the latter almost collusive. This has adversely affected our security. Training camps of the terrorists and their launching pads in Pakistan occupied Kashmir (PoK) are only a few thousand yards away. Yet we failed to carry out surgical strikes across the Line of Control in territory, which we claim to be legally ours. We did not even once exercise the right of hot pursuit across the border. We developed cold feet because we did not want another war with Pakistan on our hands. Initially, there was a fear that Pakistan had nuclear bombs in the basement. In 1999, Pakistan became a nuclear weapon state and now we could seek to justify our inaction on the plea of avoiding a nuclear war. On the other hand, Pakistan had no fears of any Indian retaliation and merrily went about pursuing its strategy of thousand cuts. Pakistan had correctly adjudged India as a soft State. Israel has been taking immediate and massive retaliatory action whenever it has been attacked from across its border. The USA sent its forces across oceans and continents in retaliation for 9/11. It is pertinent that in

2006 Prime Minister Manmohan Singh at the Round Table Conference in Srinagar talked of zero level tolerance against human rights violations but not zero level tolerance against terrorists. In an unprecedented act of appeasement, his government has provided pension benefits to the families of terrorists killed in encounter with Security Forces.

After 26/11, foreign minister Pranab Mukherjee declared that all options were open to India. The following day Prime Minister Manmohan Singh corrected him saying all options other than war were open. Our total casualties in the three and a half wars we fought with Pakistan have been less than 10,000. We have lost three times that number fighting terrorism in Kashmir. Walter Lipman's definition of national security needs reiteration: "A nation has security when it does not have to sacrifice its legitimate interests to avoid war and is able, if challenged, to maintain them by war." We continue to suffer from a Panipat syndrome and have been sacrificing our national interests at the altar of an exclusively defensive policy. Secessionist terrorism in Kashmir is essentially a product of religious fundamentalism. Apart from inflicting heavy attrition on militants, we were making progress in curbing religious fundamentalism through promoting Kashmiriyat, which stands for amity across religious divide. Religious fanatics and anti-national forces fearing losing their base raised a communal tornado over a non-issue in relation to Amarnath Yatra. The Government's inept handling and policy of appeasement resulted in a temporary setback. The unprecedented strong retaliatory agitation in Jammu, forced the government to restore status quo ante. The subsequent large voter turn out at the Assembly and

Parliamentary elections, despite threats and boycott calls, was a welcome development. However, on the media front, the Valley Press and the "secular" national media lent support to the communalists. Media management is an important requirement for counter terrorist operations. We have not done well on this score in Kashmir.

Our record of dealing with illegal migration in Assam has been bizarre. For the sake of vote bank politics, the Congress party has been encouraging illegal migration from East Pakistan/Bangladesh into Assam. In late Sixties, Governor B K Nehru and his chief minister B P Chaliha took up this matter with Delhi when the former's cousin, Indira Gandhi was in power. They were told to stop the nonsense. In his autobiography, Nehru laments, "The East Bengal Muslim was the main vote bank of the Congress party in Assam. Chaliha dating as he did from the days of the freedom struggle cherished the values of that time. But the High Command thought otherwise; the party interests were paramount." In 1993, Lt. Gen Jameel Mahmood, the Eastern Army Commander had cautioned the chief minister of Assam that if action was not taken to curb the demographic influx from across the border, the boundary of India would have to be redrawn in the East. He also represented to Army Headquarters that if the influx continued, a Kashmir type of situation would develop in Dhubri and adjacent districts of Lower Assam, abutting the narrow Siliguri corridor. Nobody heeded these warnings. To facilitate illegal migration from Bangladesh, the Congress passed the Illegal Migration Determination Tribunal Act, a special legislation for Assam only, shifting the burden of proof to establish citizenship from the individual to the State along with other such helpful measures for the illegal migrants. This gave a further impetus to the unabated influx from Bangladesh into Assam. On 10 April 1992, chief minister Hiteshwar Saikia declared in the state assembly that there were 3 million Bangladeshi illegal migrants in Assam. He came under pressure and there was a risk of his government falling. Two days later, he stated to the Press that there was no Bangladeshi migrant in Assam.

I took over as Governor of Assam in 1997, when secessionist feelings and terrorist violence were at their peak in the State. The root cause for this was the unabated influx of illegal migrants and the Congress encouraging the same for its vote bank. I submitted a 42 paged printed report to the President highlighting that this influx was not only a grave threat to the demography of the State but also to our national security. I recommended a host of measures to deal with the problem including the repeal of the IMDT Act. With the Congress in majority in the Rajya Sabha, the NDA Government could not repeal that obnoxious act. However, the Supreme Court struck down this act, extensively quoting from my report in its judgment. My report was serialized and published in all newspapers of Assam. This raised a great fervour among the people of Assam who started regarding me as their true friend. Concurrently, through co-ordinated military operations we broke the back of ULFA militancy. The Bhutanese Army wiped out their camps in Bhutan. On the development front, we installed one lakh shallow tubewells in Assam in one year, turning the State from a rice deficit to a rice surplus State.

Our psychological initiatives of projecting the three icons of Assam—Mahapurush Shankardev, Lachit Boro Phukan and Gopinath Bordoloi as national heroes through documentaries on the television had a great impact. Lachit's statue was installed at National Defence Academy, Pune and a gold medal instituted in his name for the best cadet in officer like qualities. Guwahati airport was named after Bordoloi. He was awarded a posthumous Bharat Ratna, fifty years after his death and his 11 feet bronze statue was installed in the Lok Sabha at Delhi. The cumulative effect of all these measures was that secessionist terrorism in Assam ended. Previously, ULFA militants had a 'Robin Hood' image and those killed in operations were hailed as martyrs with large crowds assembling at their funeral at which orations were delivered eulogizing their sacrifice. There was now a total reversal of public attitude towards the ULFA. Eighty-one militants were caught by villagers over a period. Half of them were lynched and the remainder handed over to the police. The local people were now witnessing surrender of ULFA and other militants to security forces appreciatively. That was the real measure of the success we had achieved in dealing with ULFA militancy that had ravaged the State for two decades. To make our success complete, I had been recommending suitable action against the two key ULFA leaders, its President Arbind Rajkhowa and its Commander-in-Chief Paresh Barua, holed up in Dacca. They had been there for nearly twenty years and they had been traveling to various foreign countries. Yet our intelligence agencies were not able to pick them up. In sharp contrast to our inability to do so, Sri Lankan intelligence agencies, in a matter of weeks, picked up from Kuala Lampur, the newly appointed LTTE chief Kumaram Pathnanatham who had succeeded Prabhakaran. We never attempted a surgical strike against terrorist camps in Bangladesh, even though there was no threat of any nuclear retaliation or even a conventional war on that account, as in the case of Kashmir.

I completed my six years as Governor of Assam and left for Jammu and Kashmir in 2003. I had the satisfaction of seeing the insurgency in Assam virtually over. During the latter part of my tenure in Assam, I had to work with a Congress chief minister. He was highly critical of me in public for my views on illegal migration from Bangladesh. To appease his vote bank, he maintained that no infiltration was taking place from across the border. With the Congress now in power at both Delhi and in Guwahati, there was a U-turn in Government policy towards the ULFA. Militants of that outfit were on the run and were surrounded by the Army in the jungles of Upper Assam. The Army was ordered to lift their encirclement and cease-fire was declared. Fruitless dialogue with the ULFA leaders through intermediaries without much credential, continued for over a year. This allowed the ULFA all the time to regroup and make up their losses. During 2005, assembly elections Congress sought ULFA's help for a price and during National Games of 2006 it is said that the ULFA was compensated for not disturbing the mega sport event. Terrorist violence has now returned to Assam but the redeeming feature is that the ULFA no longer enjoys popular support. At the conference of chief ministers in 2009, to say the least, it was amusing to find the same Congress chief minister of Assam expressing concern about terrorist violence in

Assam by HUJI, a militant communal outfit of Bangladeshis with ISI links.

The Mumbai terror attack of 26/11 was different from previous acts of terrorism in our country sponsored by Pakistan. It was a meticulously planned invasion launched and controlled by our hostile neighbour. The footprints exposed the involvement of the State agencies of Pakistan. One of the Pakistani terrorists captured alive has provided a wealth of information. This attack was a three days nightmare. It stunned the nation and virtually held it to ransom for over sixty hours. There was a stark similarity with the humiliation suffered by us in 1962. The prime minister had then confessed that he was living in a world divorced from reality. After 26/11, the prime minister apologized to the nation. In 1962, the defence minister was sacked and after 26/11, the home minister was removed. In both these cases, the total failure of the political and professional leadership stood fully exposed. The Union Cabinet was in disarray with ministers speaking in different voices.

As already mentioned, the external affairs minister declared that all options were open to India and the following day the prime minister corrected him saying that all options except war were open. Two ministers opposed SIMI being declared an illegal outfit despite its proved terrorist links. One minister wanted all Bangladeshi illegal migrants to be made Indian citizens when increasing evidence was coming for some of them having terrorist links. Another minister wanted a judicial inquiry into Batla incident in Delhi implying that it was a fake encounter. Yet another minister insinuated that Hemant Karkare the

DGP Anti-Terrorist Group was killed during the Mumbai terror attack by Hindu extremists and not Pakistani terrorists. Our professional response left much to be desired. Despite inputs available from both foreign and our own sources that a terrorist attack on Mumbai across the seafront was in the offing, the available intelligence was neither properly analyzed nor duly disseminated. No precautionary measures were taken. The attack took everyone by surprise. The NSG took over nine hours to arrive in Mumbai. The efforts of all the elements involved in the operation were not properly coordinated at the site. It took us sixty hours to eliminate ten terrorists. It was, however, very creditable that an unarmed police officer caught an armed terrorist alive. He was posthumously awarded Ashok Chakra, the nation's highest gallantry award. A redeeming feature is that the new home minister has been making earnest efforts to remove the lacunae in our preparedness for anti-terrorist operations.

Left wing extremism in the shape of Naxal terrorism has become widespread in our country. As per the home minister, 20 States, 233 districts and 2,000 police stations are affected by this menace. The prime minister is on record saying that this poses the gravest internal threat. The Naxal movement is led by people totally indoctrinated in the teachings of Marx and Mao. Presently, a Red Corridor exists form the borders with Nepal through Bihar. Thickly forested area of 7,000 square miles mostly in Chhattisgarh comprising 20,000 tribals and 237 villages has become a haven for these Naxals. They call this a liberated zone where they run a parallel government administering justice through public courts. By extortion from business persons, contractors and even government officials, they manage to raise 500 to 700 crores a year. They have been able to acquire a formidable array of modern weapons and explosives. Their total strength is nearly 20,000 underground and 50,000 overground workers. They have been carrying out spectacular strikes like looting a district police armoury carrying away 500 rifles, attacking jails to rescue colleagues and release prisoners, attacking railway stations, trains, police stations and so on. According to reliable estimates, the Naxals are responsible for 80 per cent of violence in the country.

The Naxal movement has flourished and gained momentum primarily because of bad governance and the economically deprived people being receptive to their ideology. Our intelligence gathering has been abysmally poor and coordination of operations of police forces of different states is far below the required level. In early nineteenth century, the British crushed the Thugee menace, which accounted for thousands killed on the highways every year, primarily due to excellent intelligence network organized by Colonel Sleeman. Similarly, it was through sound intelligence gathering that Sir Charles Tegart managed to eliminate the anarchist violence in Bengal in early twentieth century. Besides, poor leadership at the junior level of both the police and the paramilitary has allowed the Naxals to score repeated success inflicting heavy casualties on police officers. Police stations are the cutting edge of police administration. They have been sorely neglected. There were some 12,000 police stations in India at the time of Independence. Our population has increased more than threefold and so have complexities of policing in modern times. Armed police battalions at the Centre and in the States have increased from about 25 in 1947 to over 2,000 now. Yet the increase in the number of police stations has been very marginal and they have been neglected in terms of facilities and infrastructure. The rank structure for higher police echelons have proliferated immensely making India's police force the most top heavy in the world but there has been no upgradation in the rank of the officer in charge of police stations. Here again, the new home minister is making long overdue efforts to improve matters. Significant success has been achieved in Andhra Pradesh through a combination of development activity and effective security action against armed Naxal cadres. Isolating the Naxals from the people and destroying their combat potential, are imperative to overcome the grave internal threat to national security.

To conclude it needs to be reiterated that sound intelligence is the bedrock for success in dealing with terrorism. In the absence of good intelligence, dealing with a terrorist is like looking for a needle in a haystack. With accurate intelligence, terrorist attack can be prevented. British intelligence services to their great credit unearthed the macabre plot of Islamists blowing up seven trans-Atlantic airliners in mid-air over the Atlantic, using liquid bombs and killing thousands of passengers. Within two years, the trial of the culprits was completed and they were awarded life sentence. As for follow up action after a terrorist attack, the action taken by the US after 9/11 is a good example. Through a combination of defensive and offensive measures, it ensured that another terrorist attack does not take place in that country. Another point that needs to be stressed is that the war on terror must be fought through offensive action so that the terrorist's capability is destroyed. No war is won by only defensive action. There are four Ps, which should form part of the doctrine for counter-terrorist operations:

Political Will: Hard political decisions must be taken and under no circumstance, policy of appeasement or vote bank politics should be allowed to prevail. The latter causes paralysis in decision-making.

Professionalism: The intelligence agencies, the security forces, the administration and criminal justice system must be suitably geared to deal with this challenge, displaying high standards of professionalism.

People's support: The people should be mobilized both for providing information and for countering terrorist propaganda.

Propaganda: A terrorist fights with two weapons: the gun and propaganda. He has to be neutralized on both these fronts. Margaret Thatcher had rightly stated that the media provides oxygen to the terrorists. That oxygen must be denied to them.

9

Effectiveness and Limitations of Army in Combating Terrorism

Lt Gen DB Shekatkar, PVSM, AVSM, VSM (Retd)

At the ground level, terrorism is essentially a criminal activity; sought to be justified in pursuance of a political agenda. It should, therefore, lie primarily in the domain of police organizations, paramilitary forces (such as Border Security Force, Central Reserve Police Force, Assam Rifles, and so on), and political organizations and institutions (since many time they are seen instrumental for emergence of terrorist and violent activities as well as tendencies) to deal with. Is there a need for a military response? Assuming that deployment of military power against terrorist as a lost resort by any government, how do we judge the effectiveness of military response in combating terrorism? There are several limitations of army operations, especially when they operate in their own country, among their own people. What are these limitations? And, how do they effect counter terrorist operations?

Proxy War

In conventional war, military's role is well defined. However, for various reasons this type of conflict is becoming rare, especially where the opposing forces possess equal or matching combat power. Proxy war using terrorism as the vanguard has become favoured method of achieving political objective by nations, sub-national groups assisted by other sympathetic nations/groups. Terrorist organizations are now capable of global networking; and with sea-pirates as well as crime-syndicate, mafia groups, underworld operatives, hawala operators, drugs and weapon smugglers also active in the fray; terrorism is assuming dangerous proportions as a part of fourth generation or asymmetric warfare. With this development the very nature of warfare appears to be getting metamorphosed. The chemical, biological and nuclear technology is within the reach of non-state actors, and rogue regimes. A loose control over weapons of mass destruction, the capability in area destruction, collateral damage of improvised bombs, improvised explosive devices on use of civil aircraft, merchant ships as weapons of destruction has emerged in the form of a prohibitively risky proposition. The threat from terrorism is increasing many folds with every passing day and hence need involvement of all sections of national as well as international governing system. Military alone cannot manage it. However, armed forces, in any nation are the last resort, but such a stage comes only when the threat has developed to a dangerous level and in alarming proportion. Army all over the world will have limitations and will find it difficult to bring the situation under control in short time, expected by public and the government, specially the ill-informed and un-informed politicians and so-called NGOs.

Menace of Terrorism

India has faced terrorist violence for almost three decades now. Terrorism, as the world understands today, has been part of all conventional conflicts across the world. Today, terrorism has emerged as "philosophy of war". One may call it low intensity conflict, unconventional conflict, fourth generation warfare, proxy war, asymmetric warfare or by any other name. The fact is that today threat from terrorism is more frightening than the possibility of conventional war. Presently, everybody irrespective of gender, caste and creed is witnessing the impact and horror of terrorism. Since 2001, there has not been a single day when terrorist violence or the counter-violence by security forces is not in news. There is no country in the world today no matter how powerful militarily, which can say with confidence and with certainty that we have no threat from terrorism, extremism, or fundamentalism. No nation can claim that there will not be a terrorist attack/violence in future in that country.

Peace returns in North East

India faced and combated insurgency in North East for over four decades. Initially, it was a tribal insurgency, wherein insurgents used old, vintage means and mechanism to kill people, security forces, state police personnel with a view to terrorise people and government administration. With the passage of time and advent of new technology the insurgents of North East became techno-terrorists, posing a challenge of different kind. Insurgency in North East ended in its second phase, only due to effective and judicious use of force or military power. This included the valuable contribution by paramilitary forces, state armed police, state police, and intelligence agencies besides the active involvement and support of these very people among whom the insurgents were born, brought up and sustained. End of insurgency in Mizoram is a success story; Nagaland is comparatively peaceful; people of Manipur have realized the value of peace for development, and futility of insurgency terrorism and related violence. When the insurgency erupted and became a dangerous threat, government of India had no other option but to deploy army and other security forces to combat insurgency and violence. Indian army with the help of state and central government and with the help of people contained insurgency and brought down the violence to a level where other mechanism, initiatives, and process to establish lasting peace could commence.

Containing Terrorism

In the case of Punjab, too, the terrorism became defunct with the help of people and state police. Situation in J&K is gradually returning to normal. It may not be out of place to state that terrorism in J&K has been contained. There is a need to understand the difference between "containing terrorism" and eliminating terrorism. Army and other security forces by using force, and power can contain terrorism; however, the elimination of terrorism is possible only with the help of people and by using several other measures. "Elimination of terrorism" requires removal of the "cause" of terrorism and that can be social, economic, political and psychological. What has been happening the world over for almost a decade now, the terrorists are killed and will continue to be killed; but "we are not addressing elimination of terrorism". Terrorism is a state of mind. Concomitantly, the terrorist acts are the manifestation of the violence in minds "on ground" and among people.

Culture of Violence

Terrorist violence is born from a hurt, a wounded spirit, burned and blistered by the fire of arrogance, anger, and the desire to take revenge; a spirit splintered and frayed by the frustration of powerlessness, helplessness, a spirit parched with the thirst for a meaningful life, a spirit shrivelled and shrunk by a feeling of inferiority. The rage that results from injured self-respect, and humiliation, erupts like a volcano. (9/11; 26/11, attack on Parliament and so on). The culture of violence gives sadistic pleasure to the perpetrator. And, this culture has become pan-global, endangering the peaceful and meaningful existence of humankind.

Global terrorism, international terrorism, political terrorism, religious terrorism, cross border terrorism, or any other type of terrorism and terrorist violence represents the emerging low cost, high pay-off alternative to other known forms of transnational violence. Radicals are increasingly using it across the world as a means to project their reach and influence beyond the boundaries of national states in an attempt to pressurize the target state or target society into submission through a combination of physical violence and fear psychosis. Terrorism in its present form and future possibilities is a distinctive disorder of the modern world. It originated as a term in our lifetime and not only it has come into the spotlight of global conflict; but is also posing the biggest challenge to the peaceful existence of our human society. The present form of terrorism with its frightening reach and lethality is not only endangering the present world but is also sowing seeds for the destruction of coming generations. The stage has arrived when we feel terrified by the very idea of being terrified.

Transnational Terrorism

Terrorism has surfaced from time to time in different part of the world. Some terrorist actions are confined to a nation state or group of states within a region and sometimes these are transnational well. An analysis of Tel Aviv terrorist violence of May 1972, revealed that "a terrorist operation can be planned in Germany by Palestine Arabs, executed in Israel by terrorist recruited in Japan, trained in France, with weapons acquired in Italy (but manufactured elsewhere) supplied by Arab diplomats, with money provided by yet another Islamic country. That was in 1972—20th century. We are now in 21st century.

A complex web of interaction and relationship between terrorist organizations in different parts of the world is surfacing gradually but surely. Cooperation and connectivity between terrorist organizations sustained and indoctrinated on religious lines, their supporters, sympathizers and sustainers have increased manifolds. There is a concomitant sophistication in all modes of communication with the developments and advancements in various fields of science and technology. The 9/11 is a glaring example of meticulous planning and execution of "techno-terrorism". Many a terrorist belong to well-to-do families. They are well educated, thoroughly indoctrinated with misguided religious philosophy. The September 11, 2001 attack at the World Trade Centre and Pentagon in United States highlighted a paradigm shift in the security paradigm at the international theatre. These events underscored the vulnerability of the institution called "nation state" from a new form of a security threat from non-state actors terrorist and the new form of asymmetrical warfare called terrorism. The attacks on the train in Madrid, on London Metro, on Indian Parliament, in Mumbai local trains, and the 26/11 signify very clearly that no deterrence mechanism, be it combat power or army power can prevent terrorist attacks. The financial network supporting terrorism is very complex and sophisticated, and very difficult to detect financial sustenance coupled and connected with smuggling of weapons and drugs and the ability of the syndicates operating the mechanism to eliminate those who come in their way has resulted in "Narco-Terrorism". Terrorist organizations across the world and their supporters are sending a clear message: "we can hit you; we can kill your people wherever we want, whenever we want and with whatever mechanism, methods, means and weapons... but you do not have an effective response mechanism".

In the Indian context, it is almost impossible to bring the culprits of illegal financial transactions to book, because of loopholes in the transaction system and legal system. It is only recently that the Central Government has instituted some checks and safeguards.

Techno Terrorism

Technology has changed the world. The use of computers and mobile phones has increased manifolds in the last 20 years. Internet has become a ubiquitous tool of communication and information. Increased computing power and internet have become essential underpinning of global terrorism. It is likely that in just a few years hence there will be increased connectivity, interoperability and coordination among terrorist organizations, non-state actors, supporters and sustainers of terrorism, underworld operatives and sea pirates. It is also likely that clandestine transfer of nuclear technology and expertise will spread through communication technology. It is not very difficult to prepare and explode a chemical device. It is also possible to engineer a chemical leak in densely populated areas. No military power will be able to control this alone. We will need a very different mechanism to deal with the increased threat. Terrorism is a common challenge. Failure is not an option in our fight against terrorism, Naxalism and insurgency. We will not be able to build hope to win with military might alone. We can build it through good governance, coordinated efforts and development.

Winning the Hearts

In combating terrorism, and insurgency the numbers cannot measure the quantity of success. Statistics could be dangerous. Management techniques based on quantification models can be disastrous as we saw during Vietnam war and Soviet occupation of Afghanistan. The territorial gains are not a parameter of success (as we saw in Iraq and Afghanistan). The sole objective of the terrorists is annihilation. We must involve people to protect them. The success will come; if we can create a situation where the villagers want to work, build the roads, schools, run clinics and terrorists are the only one stopping the villagers; that will be the real success. We achieved this in Kashmir and Assam. To win a war against terrorism and insurgency we need patience. There is no possibility of quick results. As is in the case of a conventional war; it is not possible to give any period for the elimination of terrorism. Anyone who wants to claim success within a short period must be prepared to face reverses, failure and pay heavy price initially (as we experienced during IPKF operations in Sri Lanka and during the Kargil conflict).

In combating terrorism, military forces must lead by example. Indian Army's motto has always been to win the hearts and minds of people and generate hope, confidence, and faith in governing mechanism. I came across a statement of the US advisor posted in Afghanistan; the advisor said that they (NATO and the American forces) were not there to win hearts and minds. What they needed was to engender hope and faith in Afghan Government? Technically, the statement may appear to be correct; but to create an environment to combat terrorism, unless we win the hearts and minds of local population, one should not hope to engender hope and faith in that government. This is the basic principle of psychological operations in support of military operation to combat terrorism and insurgency.

Computer Terrorist Operations

We must remember that in any given area of operations or in a society, only a small fraction of youth consists of hardened terrorists who are willing to fight to death. Majority of the people, especially the youth are ordinary people with no jobs and means of sustenance. It is this situation which compels them to adopt terrorism as a profession to earn money. If given alternatives or better options, they will certainly opt for normal life to earn and live peacefully.

Another aspect of counterterrorist operation is the availability of safe sanctuary and training ground for terrorists. Success in counterterrorist operations means nothing or very little if terrorist can find safe hideouts, sanctuary, or camps in areas where forces conducting counterterrorist operations cannot operate effectively, due to political, diplomatic and international regulations/ compulsions. Indian army and other security forces combating terrorism and insurgency found themselves constrained because insurgents operating in North East India could establish camps, and get safe sanctuary in neighbouring countries like Myanmar and Bangladesh. Laldenga conducted his insurgency campaign in Mizoram for almost two decades from Bangladesh (earlier known as East Pakistan). International rules, regulations, sensitivity of neighbouring countries prevent Indian army in conducting cross border operations. Even during the Kargil war, the Indian army and Air Force could not cross Line of Control in Kargil to hit the logistic base and supply routes of intruders who Pakistan had branded as Mujahids. The situation in Kashmir is even more difficult. The terrorists operating in Kashmir not only find safe sanctuaries, safe heavens in neighbouring Pakistan occupied Kashmir, but also elsewhere in Pakistan. They also get training, weapons, equipment, financial help, indoctrination, motivation from ISI and Pakistan Army. Terrorism in India is an extension of Pakistan's foreign policy, defence philosophy and mechanism. The philosophy of bleeding India by thousand cuts is an example. Despite public demand and support in India, for conducting transborder counter terrorist operations in POK, the Government of India finds itself constrained in permitting limited and controlled counter terrorist operations. Terrorists and their supporters take full advantage of this weakness/limitation. Therefore, Indian Army's entire focus and concentration remains on guarding the line of control, plugging the routes of infiltration and exit. Increasing incidents of clashes between Indian Army and terrorists on the Line of Control during the process of infiltration are an example.

Hurdles on the Way

Situation in Afghanistan is no different. While NATO forces and the US Army can carry out effective counterterrorist operations against Taliban and al-Qaeda, they cannot operate in border areas of Pakistan. It is for this reason that a large number of terrorists and their leaders crossed over to Pakistan and established their camps and strongholds in areas like Swat and Waziristan. For various reasons the NATO forces and Afghan Army (which is better suited to conduct counterterrorist operations for various reasons that need not be discussed here) cannot conduct operations in these areas. Pakistan Army will not be effective in counterterrorist operations for various reasons. First, there is tribal linkages and tribal affinity between people staying on both sides of the border; they have age-old relations, understanding and concept of mutual existence. Second, the terrain is difficult and terrorists exploit it. Pakistan Army's troops who mostly belong to Punjab and Sindh provinces may not find it easy to operate in these areas. Pakistan Army is finding it difficult to conduct covert operations against terrorists. It is questionable if leadership in Pak Army will deploy large number of troops who belong to Baluchistan and NWFP and who are more suited to conduct counterterrorist operations in these areas for obvious reasons. Third, Pakistan Army, ISI and the government have developed expertise and mechanism to create export and sustain terrorism and insurgency in neighbouring countries and even in nations, which are far away from Pakistan. They have not developed philosophy, strategy or mechanism to combat terrorism and insurgency on their own land. Pakistan's military does not have the skills and resources to conduct an effective counter-insurgency campaign. It is a fact that when any nation, society, permits the armed forces, of uncontrolled ambition, capacity, mechanism to influence the events and environment across national borders; it is at the cost of internal security mechanism and internal defence. Was there a concept of Home Land Security in USA before the 9/11? This issue needs a serious in-depth study and debate. Fourth, there must be a sizeable element within Pakistan Army, which must be keen on continuation of terrorism in Afghanistan and even in India and China. It helps in diverting the focus of people. Creation of Mujahedeen and Taliban in Afghanistan to combat Soviet Forces in Afghanistan; spreading and sustaining of insurgency in North East India earlier through East Pakistan, and now Bangladesh, spreading and sustaining terrorism in Punjab, supporting and sustaining terrorism in J&K are examples. It is possible that on the one hand, Pakistan Army pretends to fight terrorists in Pakistan, but on the other hand, some elements within Pakistan Army as well as some other organs of the government are sustaining terrorism in Afghanistan and some parts of Pakistan's area adjoining Afghanistan. One cannot rule out the possibility of extremists and terrorists operating in China's Xingjian province may have received training in Afghanistan and Pakistan and may still be having some links. Fifth, American predator drones are used to target al-Qaeda, specially the leadership in the border areas of Pakistan, but it is at the cost of igniting and inflaming the Pushtun-led insurgency in the border areas of Pakistan, specially in Baluchistan. Baluchistan is likely to slip out of the effective control of Pakistan gradually. This development will have its own implications. Since Pakistan Government, Pakistan Army neither have the experience, nor the resources, nor strong will to combat Taliban and al-Qaeda (to retain strategic option); it is likely that Islamist elements, extremists, terrorists will find it comparatively easy to increase their influence and hold in Pakistan. They may not be able to takeover governance of Pakistan in political and diplomatic terms, (as we saw in Afghanistan), but increase in their influence and hold in Pakistan will certainly increase stakes in military terms. This may include nuclear technology and nuclear facilities (not necessarily nuclear bombs, nuclear missiles, and delivery mechanism presently under the control of Pakistan's Armed Forces) this may radically change the strategic and security environment in Central Asia, Iran, Afghanistan, India and even China. What will be the effectiveness of military power (military power of Pakistan and that of NATO and even the USA) in such a dangerous situation? We cannot and should not ignore the fact that AQ Khan's syndicate network runs deep and is still intact. The latest exposures and reports that the drug smugglers in Mexico have developed a submarine like capability and Sri Lanka's navy has discovered a submarine are a matter of serious concern. It reflects on "capability". LTTE had acquired—even limited air strike capability. All these put together can result in development of delivery mechanism. Aircraft used for artificial rain by use of chemicals can also be useful for chemical attack. What technological mechanism do terrorist suicide bombers use? Sixth, it is my experience of four decades in army service and combating insurgency, terrorism, extremism, that after certain length of time insurgency and terrorism becomes money generating, moneymaking enterprise. This is true all over the world, without an exception. Terrorism and insurgency have become cottage industry in both J&K and North East. Think of the funds allocated to these states during last 20 years. Every state demands more funds from the Central Government to combat violence. At times violence is deliberate to destroy proof. There is a well-organized system and mechanism to make money. It is equally true of the funds allocated to combat Naxalites in different states of India. Based on my experience I can state with a reasonable degree of confidence that most of the funds allocated to combat terrorism, insurgency and Naxalites are misused.

The case of Afghanistan and Pakistan is no different. Just compute the financial allocations to ISI to counter Soviet forces in Afghanistan. The funds, weapons and equipment were channelled through Pakistan. How much of it actually reached the so-called Majahideen who were fighting against Soviet Army?

If we compute the funds allocated by the USA, and Western countries to combat terrorism and insurgency in Afghanistan and Pakistan since the 9/11, the figures will be amazing. The governing mechanism of Pakistan, its army and ISI have developed expertise and sophistication to use America and other Western countries as "milch cow". All the rulers in Pakistan since 1980 without an exception have always been asking for more funds to combat the same terrorists who are a creation of Pakistan. Terrorism in Afghanistan and Pakistan is ruse to make money to develop terrorism into a well-organized cottage industry. Will the US and other patrons of Pakistan continue to give financial aid to Pakistan, if the terrorism were to end in Afghanistan and Pakistan? America will be fully justified in seeking the justification for liberal grants, loans and other methods of getting funds. When the economy of a state, a nation, of influential and powerful section of society start surviving on the funds generated on the pretext of combating terrorism and insurgency; what can be the effectiveness of military power alone?

Perils of Failure

Despite all the limitations and handicaps in the use of military power in combating terrorism, "failure in successfully combating terrorism" is not and cannot be an option in India, Afghanistan, Pakistan, and China or anywhere in the world. Failure in combating terrorism will have dangerous consequences for the entire world than the impact of dropping of nuclear bomb during World War II. If the nations all over the world do not cooperate with the USA in eliminating terrorism, which is very different from killing terrorists, and if America leaves Iraq and Afghanistan out of frustration or recurring heavy cost in all respects, the terrorists and their supporters all over the world will be encouraged. We may have to witness more 9/11, and 26/11. The terrorists will target the so-called powerful, developed, economically strong nations. The underdeveloped and poor countries may witness more internal violence by local terrorist syndicates. The terrorists will target entire Western World, the USA, Israel, India and China. If one studies and tries to comprehend the geography from Indonesia to Israel (Pacific Ocean to Mediterranean Sea, and Indian Ocean Rim); it will be very clear as to what, where, when, why and how terrorists can do what they would like to do. No military power will be able to stop them from doing so purely based on military power alone.

No one can rule out the possibility of emergence of new political identity out of Pakistan. The philosophy and process has already commenced in some parts of Pakistan, due to the spread and influence of terrorist organizations. Military power alone cannot stop it. There are limitations of usefulness and effectiveness of military power in combating terrorism, low intensity conflict and unconventional war.

The terrorists of today and of the future will be educated, sharp, technologically expert (just examine the case of ISI agent named Nadeem who was caught by police recently; his mission was to recruit engineers and IT experts for terrorist organizations) they are ingenious, thoroughly indoctrinated, trained and supported. They will find infiltration routes and avenues in Europe and the USA. They will use local, frustrated and disgruntled youth. The terrorists will receive training in launching chemical, biological and nuclear attack (not necessarily using conventional nuclear weapons and means). We must remember that if there is a wrong way to do something then someone will do the wrong way. There are reports of al-Qaeda and other militant organizations using online tools for any sinister activities. Today, the counter to global fight against terrorism is cyberspace. Availability of pictures, information on cyber network has its own implications.

Based on my personal interaction with captured and surrendered terrorists, during the command of a division in Kashmir Valley in 1995-96, I was able to get some inputs about the possibility of use of commercial aircraft as bomb against the USA. I shared these inputs during an interaction with a US delegation at New Delhi in 1997; however, the delegates did not pay any heed since the inputs were from Indian army officer. Things changed after the 9/11. A detailed account of the philosophy and possible line of action by terrorists against the USA received their serious attention in the chapter on Terrorism, authored by me. The need is to understand the reality that terrorist carry out a detailed and long-term planning for their major terrorist attack/strike.

Unlike conventional war, counterterrorist and counter-insurgency operations, quickly turn unpopular among the local population and also among political leadership (for obvious reasons) and governing mechanism, since they want quick results and are always eager to hear "good news" only. In unconventional war, "good news" is not always possible. Many time counterterrorist operations do go "badly". When the armed forces specially the army and police are asked questions which are not warranted, subjected to false and coloured propaganda, accusation of violation of human rights and so on, the rank and file who face bullets and threats every day and their leadership feel hurt, humiliated, insulted and cheated. This is more so in Indian context. Troops feel that they are doing a "thankless job". This poses serious challenge to the leadership at different levels in army, paramilitary forces, and even state police, as to how to keep the troops focused and maintain desired level of motivation, which is so crucial for success in prolonged unconventional war of peculiar nature. When the bullets fly, troops have no option but to respond and in doing so things do go wrong at time. Only seasoned commanders who have served in dangerous environment and have combated terrorism and insurgency can appreciate the problems and difficulties. Those who work in air-conditioned environment, far away from ground realities, who borrow wisdom from internet and printed articles can never appreciate and understand the compulsions of ground forces combating terrorism/ insurgency.

While it may be easy to calculate the cost of counterterrorist operations in terms of funds spent casualties to the soldiers, civil population and so on, it is very difficult to calculate cost of defeat if the counter terrorist/insurgency operations are terminated mid-way without attaining the overall strategic objective for which the operations were launched. The cost of leaving will always be larger. Return of terrorists, insurgents, or their supporters and sustainers to power; possibility of civil unrest, which may be similar to civil war like situation, destabilization of adjoining states, nations where terrorist can operate at will. Let us learn from Afghanistan episode. The biggest danger is when every terrorist, Jihadist, extremist, fundamentalist in every part of the world feels emboldened due to success of some terrorist in some part of the world.

Harsh Reality

In India, we conduct the counter terrorist operations on our land and on our national soil. The soldier combating terrorism feels that he is fighting for just cause of protecting our nation and people as well as ensuring territorial integrity. Therefore, commitment to "cause to fight for" and motivational levels are different. But when troops from a country are deployed to combat terrorism in an alien country, thousands of miles away from their own country, the motivational levels are very different. One of the basic pre-requisite for success in war of any type; is "justified cause to fight for". If the cause of prolonged conflict is not justified, the support of the local population in "combat zone" and also the support of the population of the country to which the troops belong to, will decline after a certain length of time depending on success and outcome of the conflict. This in turn may result in loosing "friends and allies". Why have some nations pulled out of Iraq and why are some eager to pull out from Afghanistan? How to keep the forces of different nations united and focused in combat zone is the biggest challenge to any theatre commander. No political leader, diplomat, bureaucrat and even senior armed forces commander—the so-called experts—who have never faced the ground realities, will agree with my views, but this has always been, and will always remain a bitter truth and a harsh reality.

We must Win

Finally, we must always remember the age-old reality that "insurgents and terrorists do not win a war, but their opponents often lose it"! As I explained earlier, there is no scope for any nation across the world to lose war against terrorism. Defeat is not the military option. We must also remember, "The weak but determined have one weapon, the error of those who think they are strong".

There is a need to send clear-cut message across the world: "Do not believe in the alliance of money and machine gun, because your children will inherit not the money, but the machine gun, which will not only destroy the children but everyone else".

If we can send the above message through several means and mechanism, we can hope to establish peace. Because no child is born as a terrorist—terrorists are created and sustained. Military power alone has its limitation in winning war against terrorism.

10

Financial Terrorism

BR Lall, IPS (Retd)

Financial terrorism impinges directly on national security and affects adversely the defence of the country. Terrorism and the terrorist are much dreaded words, apparition of which chills the spine as one starts perceiving death hovering around. The terrorists may have noble or ignoble reasons or ends but its consequence—the instant violent death, evokes extreme fear.

Physical terrorism in various forms that we normally see like religious, regional, racial, separatist or Naxalism are some of the commonest visible apparent forms terrorism takes. These may have bearing on a region, a community, or a group for some time and may be resolved, but the financial terrorism is continuous, it is universal in all regions and in all spheres of life all over the country. Wherever somebody is being deprived of his due under force, fear, blackmail or coercion, the exploiter is none other than a financial terrorist and financial terrorism is in operation. More the exploitation, the higher is the degree of terrorism.

Financial terrorist adopts many ways to loot and exploit the people down the line. The simplest is tax evasion but may also include crimes like dacoities, black-marketeering, adulteration in medicines and foodstuffs; counterfeiting currency, money-laundering, spurious billing; blackmailing, non-payment of full wages, economic exploitation of women, children, illiterates and other helpless groups; under and over invoicing in imports and exports, not depositing the PF of employees; besides these corruption of any kind like benami transactions etc. Briefly, financial terrorists extort money from persons of all hues.

The various forms of physical terrorism correspond to the cause they ostensibly fight for namely religion, regionalism, ethnicity, separatism, and depravity/ exploitation. The whole world is affected by terrorism of one of the first four types and the terrorists have perfected the art of ingraining the worst possible fear among the innocent mass of population. Another type of terrorism is emerging in India i.e. terrorism by the depressed over their exploiters as perhaps a reaction. Naxalism and bulk of violent property crime is more in the nature of reaction to the financial terrorism. They are the people who the terrorists have driven to the wall. They have no access to education, sanitation, health services, and they do not receive the minimum wages as enacted by law. If they rise against this exploitation and demand justice, they are suppressed and if they take to violence, they are branded as terrorists. As such, the effects of financial terrorism are much greater and far more serious than the physical terrorism. The violence that these exploiters inflict may manifest itself into the various forms like hunger, disease, depravity that leads ultimately to slow death at mass scale. It is a sort of genocide caused by monetary manipulations or through financial operations. Non-payment of wages even at the minimum rate directly deprives the deserving people of all the necessities, but basically any diversion of the wages into the unaccounted sector in any way amounts to an activity of the financial terrorist. When some group combines physical fears along with any of the above, it is termed as mafia. All mafias are financial terrorists first and they employ physical terrorism in order to perpetuate their financial terrorism.

Role of Public Servants

In the final analysis, it is the public servants who nurture and sustain this financial terrorism. There are laws to tackle all such activities, as all these are defined as crime but it is the corruption by the public servant at all levels of bureaucracy, professions, judiciary and politicians right up to the ministers that forbids any action against them. In India since no denominations and levels are free from corruption, so all of them are conspirators and abettors in this crime of genocide by the financial terrorism. There is no invoking of law when it is likely to affect the higher ups. If some laws fall inadequate, there is no attempt to amend the lacunary provisions of such laws. They do not allow the Lokpal Bill to move, as that will jeopardize the politicians. It is not possible for the enforcement agencies to act against the high and mighty within the existing legal parameters. I have written at length on this subject in my work 'Who Owns CBI: The Naked Truth'. The rules of business are such that law-enforcing agencies can take no initiative on their own and have to look up to those who they want to investigate. This is why no scam has had a rendezvous with its logical conclusion, for the simple reason that the evidence is willfully scuttled. Further, the buck does not stop at that. If the supreme court in Jain Hawala case ruled for equal treatment to all and declared the provisions related to the special permission for investigating higher level public servants as discriminatory and ultra vires the constitution, the government reacted by making inbuilt provisions in the CVC Act of 2003 that no officer of the rank of joint secretary and above will be proceeded against without the permission of the government, i.e. the same Executive as is accused of and is being investigated for corruption, as if it is duty bound to safeguard the higher ups by hook or by crook. Any number of such examples can be cited. The government enacts laws conducive to corruption. The financial terrorists need money and the pliable laws enacted by the government help them amass money—the infrastructure of the financial terrorism. In a book release function at the India International Centre, the most pious intellectual place in the Capital, one former minister narrated that he was to attend a Cabinet meeting scheduled at PM house; he reached a little early and entered into discussions with the prime minister. The minister, who had reputation for straight and honest dealings, advocated an enactment of a law on forfeiture of the assets of those involved in corruption cases. During the discussions, others also entered and participated in the discussion. Barring just one more minister, all others virtually revolted against the idea and expressed not only strong reservation but also very strong sentiments including the threat of leaving the coalition/cabinet. The prime minister, who was listening to the discussions, quietly gave a sarcastic smile to the minister who had raised the issue and remarked, "Is Mahfil Ke Kaide Kanoon samajh Lejie, Aap bhi Iska Hissa Hain". (You had better understand the way this coalition likes to go as you are also a part of it).

The worst perpetrators of financial terrorism are the officers of higher echelons who indulge in all sorts of financial irregularities even as disallowing any investigations against them. It is now a well-known fact that corruption has contaminated every level, every profession and every service. The big three i.e. the bureaucrats, the politicians and the judges try not to be accountable at all. They create a protective shield around themselves to remain free from any accountability. Some are able to arrange such provisions directly because of the power of the state they enjoy. Others exercise influence and the rest are able to pay their way through, but ensure that they become inaccessible for all their misdeeds. My perception of each one of the big three is as follows:

Bureaucrats

1. They issued a directive not to proceed against any senior bureaucrat unless his own peer group permitted and they decided among themselves not to grant any such permission. The vested interest and the built-up is so strong that when the Supreme Court hit down this provision as discriminatory and ultra vires the statute and the constitution, the same

was notified as an ordinance. The ordinance was withdrawn due to the pressure of public opinion. Subsequently, it was enacted as a provision in the CVC Act and stands on the statute book.

2. The investigations i.e. the collection of evidence is not allowed as all the investigating/enforcement agencies are under the same executive who indulges in corruption. The financial terrorist himself directs the investigation and collection of evidence. All these processes are still born.
3. Prosecution sanction is another constituent of this Lakshman Rekha that does not allow any action against these big financial terrorists. It is strange that now, even the Lakshman Rekha is being drawn by the Ravan and not by Lakshman.
4. If in a case all these stages are crossed, still there is another obstacle that has to be crossed before the case can be taken to logical end and that is the provision of withdrawal. As agents of the state, they can withdraw any case in public interest. It has the discretion to define anything or any process as 'in public interest'. Thus, even the final withdrawal is in the name of the exploited masses. In other words, in the name of the country as if corruption is for the benefit of public.

Politicians

Whereas all the above protections are applicable in case of politician also, he protects himself further in other forms as well.

1. The politicians have exempted themselves from any bar in fighting election even when convicted for a period of less than two years. For dealing with

conviction for three years or more, he takes protection under the judicial dictum that nobody is guilty until proved by law. The provision was built in the law in context of the criminals so that the society does not maltreat them in the intervening period. However, nowhere has the law or the constitution conferred any right on the criminals to rule. If law holds somebody as criminal after ten years or twenty years, imagine the havoc he would have wrought during this intervening period. In any case, we do not deserve to be ruled by the shady characters suspected of being criminals; we deserve to be ruled by the fairest of the fair.

2. The politicians subordinate the enforcement agencies and refuse to provide functional independence to any of the existing agency or create an independent agency that will not be subordinate to them and that could suo moto take up cases of misconduct against them. All countries have created ombudsmen under whatever nomenclature it may be. However, in India there is a great resistance for creating such an institution like Lok pal, as the politicians in India do not want any enquiries against them by any independent authority. Therefore, they do not allow the enactment of the Lokpal as all of them will have to be accountable to Lokpal. In the case of shady politicians, which most of the politicians are, an enquiry against such a politician will expose his misdeeds before the public.
3. All over the civilized world, the investigating agencies are free but not in India. Deciding the respective roles of the Police commissioner, Lord

Denning, the Chief Justice of UK, in 1986 delivered his judgment whose operative part is as follows:

"I have no hesitation, however, in holding that, like every constable in the land he should be, and is, independent of the executive. He is not subject to the Orders of the Secretary of State, I hold it to be the duty of the Commissioner of Police, as it is of every chief constable, to enforce the law of the land. He must take steps so as to post his men that crimes may be detected; and that honest citizens may go about their affairs in peace. He must decide whether or not suspected persons are to be prosecuted; and, if need be, bring the prosecution or see that it is brought; but in all these things he is not the servant of anyone save of the law itself. No Minister of the Crown can tell him that he must, or must not, keep observations on this place, or that; or that he must, or must not prosecute this man or that one. Nor can any police authority tell him so. The responsibility for law enforcement lies on him. He is answerable to the law and to the law alone".

Despite the recommendations of the National Police Commission in 1980 and the Supreme Court ruling to that effect in 2007, the government has not given the investigating agencies an inch of their space. One wonders whether we are part of the civilized modern world or we are living in the dark middle ages when all the powers were vested in the arbitrary discretion of the king and his friends.

Both these categories are given the following further protection.

a) Whenever there is investigation against the VIPs, the same are not allowed to be conducted with all sorts of spokes put in the wheels. If you fail to collect any evidence, no evidence comes on record and this is enough to drop the case. Further, if investigations were required abroad, the letter rogatory would be rather impossible to get. It is for the court to issue letter rogatory, but the government has to give an undertaking of reciprocity without which the letter is meaningless. The Government can go to any extent. In 1994, the government withdrew the CBI power to apply to the court for letter rogatory. Normally, this power vests with the SHO. To block the CBI from applying in the court, the government centralized it in the PMO.

b) Ultimate, of course, the prosecution sanctions which is a salient feature of corruption laws in India provides that unless the executive permit, there can be no prosecution of the accused.

The Judge

The Judges behave like men from moon as if they owe no accountability to anyone, not even to their own hierarchy. They refuse to respond to any checks, accountability or discipline. This is true in particular of the higher judiciary, i.e. the high courts and the Supreme Court.

1. They do not want to submit themselves to any enquiry whatsoever by any state agency nor would take any action within their own set-up. There have been a number of such cases; the latest is the UP Provident Fund Scam.

2. According to the Supreme Court order, nobody can register a case against a judge even if he is accused of patent criminality. The question is that should the judges be immune from liability for their criminal acts. The UP Provident Scam brought this issue to the fore. Though they had misappropriated the money belonging to their own subordinates from their provident funds, or drawn fraudulently from the treasury, but still they would refuse any and every action. Thanks to Chief Justice Gokhale of Allahabad High Court, that he constituted an enquiry, under Rama Jain, the vigilance judge of the High Court that the facts came out, but then there was great resistance against any police officer taking down their statements or undertaking investigations. This is the feudal mindset as whatever be the rank of the police officer, he represents the law and they have trivialized the law in the process violating their own dictum "Be you ever so high, the law is above you". The judiciary is itself to blame for preventing law to act against the protectors of law. New rules were ordered for investigating the case against the high judicial dignitaries. The rules mandated that there would be no interrogation of the judicial dignitary. Instead, the judicial dignitary will reply at his convenience to the pre-approved questionnaire—pre-approved by the Supreme Court! It took at least two PILs to make the judiciary realize that everybody is equal before the law.
3. There has been great resistance among the judges in declaring their assets. There can be no reason or rationale for a judge not to declare his assets.

Moreover, how the declaration of assets will interfere in the independence of the judiciary? This is beyond comprehension. Rather, the provision of declaration of assets should be more stringent for judiciary and the enforcement agencies.

4. Judges refuse to be accountable for the delays in the system of justice. Worst is that they refuse to look into the causes of delays either themselves or allow any expert agencies from outside to analyze for them. While this author was serving in CBI, he attempted an analysis for the Jabalpur exclusive court of CBI. The judge was cooperating in cutting down the delays and the results were tremendous. Against the annual average disposal of 1.5 cases, it ultimately rose to as high as 46, i.e. by 3,000 per cent. Judiciary refuses to look into its obsolete processes that it had followed over the centuries and refuses to curtail on its vacation for which also there is no justification except the feudal luxury at the cost of the people. Therefore, even if some other countries may be allowing such vacation, there is no justification here, as the judiciary in India gets earned and other leaves and holidays, which are not available in other countries. Moreover, when work is lying pending to the unfathomable extent, they should work overtime, rather than indulge into the luxury of vacation. However, the judiciary following the 120th report of the Law Commission has taken one single argument that number of judges in India is much lower as percentage of population when compared with the USA, so pendency is natural. There could not be a more flawed reasoning as the workload of

judiciary is not a function of population but the cases coming to the courts for adjudication. In the USA, the number of filings per judge is many times more than in India. The Law Commission itself was not very sure about the criterion it adopted at that time. Why does the judiciary not get the whole problem looked into by an expert agency? That will make it appear accountable to the people or the law. In its worry to ward off accountability, the judiciary does not want to come under the RTI in any form as a transparent organization. The judiciary should put everything about itself on its website except any information that may affect the course of justice.

The Businessmen

The business persons, the industrialists and other groups with money bribe their way to immunity from law and indulge in financial terrorism freely. They also collaborate with the bureaucrat or the politician who arranges protection through his influence.

What matters is that all these aberrations of either category ultimately facilitate financial terrorism. A start is necessary to hold them accountable under such provisions of law that should compel them to submit to law for the maximum collection of taxes. Against tax collection of 36 per cent of the GDP in the OECD countries, India collects just 17 per cent that too on the accounted income. Since there is a parallel economy of the same size, our real collections thus slump down to a mere 8.5 per cent only. No wonder that lots of our money flows into black channels in India and abroad about which various estimates exist. Experts estimate that the size of the black economy equals the unaccounted money that is siphoned abroad. The annual outflows are nearly $ 27 billion or Rs. 1.21 lakh crores. The figure of unaccounted money siphoning is the subject of debate and controversy. During elections, the figure of $1456 billion (Rs. 70 lac crores) made headlines, though the estimates vary up to $ 7000 billion (Rs. 350 lac crores). This overwhelming expenditure on elections is no myth; it is a reality. Take the case of Hassan Ali: a stud-farm operator from Pune who was discovered by the enforcement directorate to own a Swiss Bank account. He had 8.1 billion dollars or Rs. 35,000 crores. Hassan Ali is not a lone instance; there would be hundreds and thousands Hasan Alis in India. If there were a thousand Hassan Alis—not surprising— it would mean that India has 8.1 trillion dollars stashed in secret tax havens abroad.

If we were efficient and honest, our tax collection in the past financial year will have touched 34 lakh crores. It was not so, the tax collection was just eight and a half lakh crores. The countries like the USA jealously guard any flight of capital abroad. In the USA, they discovered flight of capital and the resultant loss of taxes to the extent of 19 billion dollars in May 2008. The Internal Revenue Service started their enquiries immediately. In June 2008, the House Committee took up the leads, and began its investigations. By 31 July 2008, the reports were ready and they started acting on the same. By the month of August, they reached the conclusion that the Swiss Banks were the main culprits in aiding and abetting that evasion. That is how the USA confronts capital flight from its country.

As against the USA, we have neither the will nor the infrastructure at home to enable us to raise an effective fight, nor the international standing. The Swiss banks no wonder have rebuffed our efforts as witch-hunt and fishing expedition. The world knows our reluctance as was demonstrated in the LGT case. The German government had announced that it had a list of bank accounts of people from many countries who maintained secret bank accounts with LGT in Liechtenstein. India was one of those countries whose citizens held accounts there. Germany was prepared to give information on official request. India remained insouciant and did not make any effort to book the culprits.

There is urgent need to collect due taxes and to pull the economy out of the morass that it has been mired into. Imagine what wonders can happen in our country if tax collections rise to Rs. 34 lac crores. There is need for stringent measures to plug the loopholes and to enforce the laws with strictness. If scores of other countries of the world have achieved that, why can't we?

A number of steps can be suggested that can effectively achieve the desired results, but that would be a separate subject of study by itself. In brief, some of these are as follows:

First, reduce cash transactions in the economy and encourage use of plastic money or the banking instruments. For that, the government can set a limit for the cash transactions. Second, withdraw the higher denomination notes. Third, the government should impose heavy penalties for the tax offenders. Besides, the government should deal with such offenders with an iron hand. Fourth, treat the tax evasion beyond a certain limit as a criminal offence providing a jail term. Fifth, give independence of action to investigating agencies to proceed against the people in high places. Sixth, the penalties for the so-called elites should be more stringent. Seventh, the government should create a central registration cum accounting system to record all the property transactions. That will put a near stop to benami transactions.

If we want to achieve internal peace and generate resources for external security, we have to tackle the financial terrorists. All other forms of terrorism appeal to a limited section of society. The terrorism of nineties was limited to Punjab; the ULFA is limited to Assam; the religious struggle is limited to only parts of those sections, but the reaction against the financial terrorism that has manifested in various provinces of India in the form of Naxalism is widespread covering as many as 233 districts. Second, the young resent the exploitation by the financial terrorists. If financial terrorism remains unchecked, the country will be permanently embroiled in continuous violence. Presently, it is spreading very fast. In 1990, only 16 districts of India were affected and now the number is no fewer than 233. Let us not wait for it to spread it to any more.

11

Intelligence for Security

DC Pathak, IPS (Retd)

Security, by definition, is protection against covert attacks of the enemy. We have our defence forces to deal with any open attack on our territory. In today's environment the challenge of safeguarding the nation's integrity falls in a big way on the country's security set up for the responsibility of unravelling the clandestine plans and preparations of the enemy, external or internal, to attack Indian targets by surprise. These threats translate into acts of terrorism, destruction of our economic assets of strategic value and the sabotage of our critical information systems.

The security scenario is never static as the Indian context amply demonstrates. Some of the major threats that India faced after Independence have begun to fade away while newer challenges have arisen on the security front particularly in the post-cold war era. Regional separatism, it may be recalled, threatened India's integrity in the 1960s when the anti-Hindi agitation propelled by the Dravidian movement[1] was at its peak, called for separation of that region from the North. It is a tribute to the evolution of democratic process in India that this movement was assimilated into the national mainstream. Some of the insurgencies of the North-East seeking to assert their tribal or ethnic identities, likewise assented to accept the electoral route to empowerment even as some others have remained virulent for various reasons including the fact that support and guidance comes to them from across our borders.

Communal disharmony was the sequel of the Partition, which resulted in recurring riots sparked off by local provocations at least till the Eighties by which time the assertion of secular polity on one hand and the fading away of first hand memories of the Partition riots on the other, had reduced the intensity and frequency of this kind of violence. The demolition of Babri Masjid[2] in 1992 and the Gujarat riots of 2002 have deepened the political divide on communal lines and created a new sensitivity around the basic issue of how secularism—a natural plank of democracy in a multi-lingual and multi-religious country like India would be practised in this country. The communal front challenges the domestic peace and stability particularly as it is to an extent vulnerable to the machinations of the external adversary next door. Many of the acts of cross-border terrorism perpetrated by Pakistan on India in recent years were designed to cause communal disharmony here.

Today, terrorism is on top of our security agenda as

it is a threat emanating from across our borders and orchestrated by the Pak army and the ISI with the intention of destabilizing India. At one level terrorism is a methodology adopted by the insurgent groups in the North-East as well as by the Naxalites in the hinterland of India. It is the threat of cross-border terrorism instigated by Pakistan, however, that was to become the biggest security concern for India. Taking advantage of the success of the anti-Soviet armed campaign in Afghanistan, Pakistan decided to unleash a proxy war against India in the early nineties anchoring it on cross-border terrorism. It goes to the credit of Indian Intelligence that by 1993-94 itself, it had completely unravelled the blue-print of this new covert offensive of the Pak ISI. The proxy war had three well-defined components. One was a conscious replication of the Afghan Jihad in Kashmir by diverting the surplus of Mujahideen from the Afghan front to the Valley. This is how the Hizbul Mujahideen, the militant front of the Jamaat-e-Islami Pakistan reorganized the struggle in Kashmir on the slogan of Jihad and the first foreign Mujahideen made his appearance in Kashmir in the winter of 1994. The second plank of the proxy war was to extend terrorism beyond J&K to other parts of India and begin a new offensive in which metros like Delhi and Mumbai would be targeted and terror strikes would be carried out on big markets and places of religious significance. The objective of the proxy war was to cause internal destabilization and mount pressure on India to yield on Kashmir. The third component of the covert offensive was to use the soft borders of India with Nepal and Bangladesh to infiltrate agents to organize terrorist modules and execute the plans. 26/11 was the culmination of a slew of terrorist attacks that were planned and executed by the Pak ISI beginning from the serial bomb blasts at Mumbai in 1993.

A major threat in the current security scenario for India is the rapid rise of the Maoist movement over the last decade. Ever since the two major Naxalite groups[3]—the Maoist Communist Centre of Bihar and the People's War Group of Andhra Pradesh planned in 1994 to merge organizationally and operationally by getting connected through the Dandakaranya forest belt passing through Orissa and Madhya Pradesh—the movement spread fast on the ground steadily enlarging its arsenal and cadre strength. Presently it holds sway in 116 districts spread across a dozen states of India, having accounted for the killing of 455 civilians and security personnel in 1128 incidents so far. The Naxalites work through a large underground organization backed by numerous open forums that seek to spread the Maoist ideology. The Naxalite movement is rooted in a mix of ideological pull, harbouring of lumpen[4] elements and an unfortunate trend of the local administration withdrawing from the field in many of the affected districts. The problem calls for 'a return to the districts' and a competent handling of the security- development interface there even as sequentially the restoration of security would come first.

Thus if we take an overview, it would be clear that the biggest threats facing India's security at present are terrorism, Naxalism and communalism. Terrorism is instigated from across our border, Naxalism is so far indigenous but has the potential of acquiring a foreign umbilical cord while communalism is a domestic threat that foreign interested forces would be tempted to exploit for causing internal confusion in India. All these threats have covert dimensions and therefore need to be tracked with intelligence for pre-emptive action. When a threat has covert origins the security setup needs to have arrangements for getting prior information about the sources of these threats and the details of the enemy's plans. Intelligence by definition is the information about the covert plans of the adversary and this is precisely the reason why Intelligence is the chief weapon of security.

A few basics about Intelligence bear repetition. Intelligence must be reliable and specific enough to invite action. It must come in time so that the purpose of neutralizing the threat can be achieved. Security is preventive but as all threats cannot be defeated and the enemy may succeed in executing some of the plans, it becomes equally important to have strong post-event responses. Success in tracing and punishing the perpetrators sends out the message of deterrence to the adversary. The success of the security setup, however, is judged primarily from its ability to preempt the covert moves of the enemy on the strength of intelligence.

Intelligence is a commodity that is not available on the shelf; it requires a dedicated effort, use of skills of tradecraft and of course adequate resources. In the wake of 26/11 the Government of India has taken several measures like installation of four new hubs of the NSG at the metropolitan cities of Mumbai, Kolkata, Chennai and Hyderabad, creation of the NIA to solely investigate cases of terrorism and establishment of a nodal authority in each state to coordinate follow up action after an event.

Strengthening the Intelligence setup however is even more important. Since intelligence on the same threat comes from more than one agency, it has to be ensured that none of it is lost in transit and the total information available on the threat travels up to the action taking authority at the higher levels. The nation has to invest a lot more on Intelligence.

It is relevant to examine the role of Intelligence specifically in the context of the three prime threats viz terrorism, Naxalism and communalism facing India at present. The terror threat is in fact the threat of the proxy war that Pakistan unleashed on India with the instrumentality of cross-border terrorism. Once this was understood the intelligence tasks suggested themselves. Stepping up collection of external intelligence about the activities of the Pak army and the ISI in relation to India, focusing on Jammu & Kashmir, intensifying vigilance on Indo-Nepal and Indo- Bangladesh borders, watch on the coasts and looking for possible collaborators and 'sleepers' on our own soil, emerged as the new tasks for our Intelligence agencies. Since this would involve extending the network of informants at the grassroots as well, the proxy war threw up a very large role for the state intelligence or even the local intelligence units of the districts in safeguarding national security. It took sometime for the Centre to get the states to realize this and reorient their special branches for handling the new responsibility. The unloading of more than a thousand kilograms of RDX by boat on the Raigarh coast before the 1993 Mumbai blasts had brought out the importance of state and district police having a network of informers in the coastal settlements. The experience of 26/11 proved that our intelligence was overall deficient.

The Naxalite movement which mercifully is indigenous in character so far, raises even more sharply the issue of utilization of the enormous Intelligence resources of the states and the districts for the cause of national security. The movement is centrally directed by leaders who run a classical underground apparatus operating across the several states. It has reached the stage of 'mass actions' in which there are enough cadres and followers at the local level to rally round in hundreds to carry out clandestine attacks on police stations, jails and railway establishments, under the guidance of a few leaders who might have come in from outside. Laying an ambush and blowing off police vehicles with landmines is a kind of operation that is typically planned and executed locally within a district. It is obvious therefore that the Central agencies should be focusing on tracking the central and state leadership of the movement while the state special branches and district Intelligence units should be penetrating the network down below, to produce actionable intelligence. Too much time has been lost in the buck- passing that the states indulged in by taking the plea that Naxalism was a national security issue. In the process the states even allowed a virtual withdrawal of police and civil administration from the affected areas much to the advantage of the Maoists. The only effective strategy of dealing with Naxalism now is to concentrate on freeing a selected number of districts of this menace by reinforcing the police stations there with a company each of the armed police and reopening the territory for development. This will break the contiguity of the hold of Maoism on the ground, make it more difficult for the Naxalites to operate and gradually wean the people away from their influence. This will happen only if a lot of intelligence is produced within each affected district.

On the debilitating problem of communalism the primacy of local intelligence has always been there in the matter of preventing disorders and riots. The country has accepted the view that public life in a democracy should be kept free of any open utterances that could provoke communal ill-will. A more meaningful enforcement of the stringent provisions of law created by the Criminal Law (Amendment) Act of 1972 is needed now. Intelligence agencies of course have to keep track of the organized activities of communal outfits but the basic responsibility of watching the communal front falls on the local administration particularly as the communally sensitive pockets in the country have already been identified.

In the light of the above, three strategies of security suggest themselves in the Indian context. One is the enormous need for generating 'intelligence from below' with the help of State SBs and LIUs to complement the effort of the national intelligence agencies to deal with the major threats to internal security identified earlier. Creating an oversight mechanism at the Centre to ensure that intelligence production picks up fast in the concerned states, is extremely important. Top officials of IB may have to be assigned a cluster of states each to oversee this build-up. The central funding of the state and district intelligence agencies may have to be arranged. The districts may be identified for urgent attention. These will include those that are engulfed by Naxalism, the ones that are on the vulnerable stretch of our border and the coast and those which have sensitive communal pockets. Outside of the annual conference of the DGsP of the States, the DIB now holds regional meetings of the police and intelligence chiefs as well and this is the forum where consolidation of intelligence production should be discussed in specific terms for an identified threat.

The second strategy of security relates to the threat of cross- border terrorism that has after 26/11 drawn attention once again to the fact that the adversary across our western border has continued to pursue its proxy war against India and has even enlarged its scope to include targeting of our economic and strategic assets for terrorist strikes. The Pak army has manoeuvred the triangular equations between the US, India and Pakistan in a manner that it can get away with its covert offensive against India by passing on the blame for it to 'non-State' players or on the non- resolution of the Kashmir problem and yet manage to keep on the right side of the US policy makers. The US needs Pak army to fight its battle against the Islamic radicals represented by the al-Qaeda-Taliban axis and therefore tends to accept the plea of denial of Pak army so far as the attacks on India are concerned. What makes this happen is the fact that India is targeted by the forces led by Hizbul Mujahideen and Lashkar-e-Toiba which are under the influence of the Pak ISI right since the days of the Afghan war and which have never attracted notice for attacking any Western targets.

The spectrum of militancy in Pakistan has to be closely studied and understood by our security set-up. The oddness of India's stand at Havana in 2006 putting India and Pakistan on the same side of the fence as victims of terrorism came out in bold relief through 26/11. Even if India's policy stance was to be interpreted as a huge gesture of generosity designed to serve the cause of Indo-Pak peace process at that time, it did ignore the reality of our long standing security assessment about the proxy war that had been kept up by Pakistan even after the Kargil episode. A more significant point in this, however, is that an understanding of the character of cross- border terrorism would make it easier for the right thinking people to keep terrorism from getting enmeshed in community questions on our own home front, something that has the potential of jeopardizing our domestic policy. Terrorism is instigated from across our borders and even if some agents are won over by the adversary to join in, it does not detract from the fact that the terrorist acts are the doings of individuals who cannot be allowed to disturb communal peace and harmony. The security and police agencies will have to be extremely careful in their counter-terrorism operations to make sure that no innocent individual was touched by them. In a country where the communal problem has been a part of the legacy of Partition it becomes all the more important that the threat of cross- border terrorism is vigorously pursued but handled with a totally secular mindset.

Last but not the least, we have to have a strategy in place that allows public-private partnership to grow in the sphere of safeguarding national security. Ever since Warren Christopher, President Bill Clinton's Secretary of State enunciated in 1993 that 'economic security is inseparable from national security' this is a universally accepted doctrine and one that holds special significance for India in the scenario that the country is facing today.

Leading corporate houses can join in for bringing about technological and systemic upgradation of policing and security in the metropolitan cities as part of their CSR contribution. An aware public and credible NGOs can be the instruments for providing meaningful feed-back relatable to security, to the concerned authorities. Public awareness is important also in the context of the Naxalite threat that calls for a competent handling of the 'security-development interface'. Maoists thrive on lack of development. Security therefore has to establish an environ of security in which the message of development can be taken to the remote and tribal areas. It is however equally important that seepage of funds meant for development schemes is monitored at the district level and the institution of Collector strengthened to handle this responsibility. Prime Minister Dr. Manmohan Singh could not have expressed himself more strongly when he once said that corruption is a threat to national security.

ENDNOTES

1. Dravidian Movement: Originated in several successive social and political formations in Tamilnadu, Southern India. E. V. Ramaswamy Naicker popularly known as Periyar in Tamilnadu, disillusioned with the Congress Party that he believed was dominated by Brahmans (uppercast Hindus), founded his Self-Respect Movement in 1925 to assert the dignity of non-Brahmans, and joined hands with the Justice Party only to take over its leadership. In 1944 he rechristened it Dravida Kazhagam and crystallized its objectives. The objectives were mainly rejection of Brahman domination in all spheres of life, rejection of Aryan and northern domination over the south, rejection of all things associated with Brahmans and the north, such as Hindi, Sanskrit, Hinduism, and the paraphernalia of worship, creation of an

independent Dravidanadu i.e. Dravidian land, reversion to Tamil culture and ethos as reflected in the old Sangam literature and regaining the glory of Tamil history and language.

2. The Babri Mosque or Babri Masjid or Mosque of Babur was a mosque in Ayodhya, constructed by Babur, the first Mughal emperor of India in the 16th century. Before the 1940s, the mosque was called Masjid-i-Janmasthan ("mosque of the birthplace"). The mosque stood on Ramkot ("Rama's fort") Hill (also called Janmasthan ("Birthplace"). It was destroyed by Hindu nationalists, on December 6, 1992 despite a commitment to the Indian Supreme Court that the mosque would not be harmed.
3. Naxalite or Naxalism is an informal name given to communist groups that were born out of the Sino-Soviet split in the communist movement in India. Ideologically they belong to various trends of Maoism. Initially the movement had its centre in West Bengal. In recent years, they have spread into less developed areas of rural central and eastern India, such as Chhattisgarh and Andhra Pradesh through the activities of underground groups like the Communist Party of India (Maoist).
4. Lumpen, of or pertaining to disfranchised and uprooted individuals or groups, especially those who have lost status: the lumpen bourgeoisie.

12 The Psychology of Terrorism and Counter Terrorism Strategies

Dr Prateep V Philip, IPS

Every citizen is a stakeholder in today's terror scenario, just as the police have no time to relax or take lightly the threats that are just too many. We have been campaigning against terror with the "Friends of Police" FoP concept (a platform for such concerned and involved citizen stakeholders). The FoP has, however, not caught the imagination of police leaderships countrywide as it should, though ironically it is the only available international blueprint for community policing.

To quote another experienced police officer from Delhi, "FoP is none other than formal nomenclature to an age-old concept of basic community involved policing that empowers the individual to be part of the overall policing in which he has a stake where he can be the eyes and ears of the system and share the 'Intelligence' privy to him without suspicion of the others involved."

The recent Mumbai blasts reinforce the conviction that the war against crime, social injustice, terror, et al is not a leader's war but a people's war. The need to mobilise vast masses of citizens and all stakeholders is the only permanent deterrent. I realized this as a young police officer after surviving with severe injuries in the world's first Human Bomb that killed the former Prime Minister Shri Rajiv Gandhi in Sriperumbudur and thereafter conceptualised the concept of Friends of Police and Factor X—a proactive thought process that starts with the assumption that Factor X or the threat is not just imminent but is present and we, meaning all stakeholders or all whose life is at stake, need to do everything possible to unearth and eliminate the Factor X.

An amphibious multi-factor X attack such as the one that occurred in Mumbai on 26/11 was not a mere act of terrorism but asymmetric warfare requiring not just preparation of the police or its antiterrorist component but the army, navy and air force as well as the fire service, private security agencies and the wider public.

Constant visualisation by all these agencies of possible future asymmetric warfare scenarios is the first step in such preparation for, to be forewarned is to be forearmed. The frontlines of warfare are no longer national boundaries but crowd centres and symbols of prestige, power, affluence and national security lying deep within our domestic territory. It calls for a reorientation of the deployment of the defence forces of the country such that the crack units of the army, navy, air force, police, paramilitary are not just deployed to guard the borders but also all such installations.

The surprise element is all about extending the frontline deeper and on a more spectacular scale than has ever happened before. Lateral thinking and imagination (examples 9/11 and Maximum Terror, 26-29 November, 2008) is being used by our querries, the agents of asymmetric warfare while security agencies are operating on a precedent-driven paradigm of thinking, acting and reacting to what has happened before.

After the idea of Friends of Police Movement won the prestigious 15000 pounds, Her Majesty the Queen's Award for Innovation in Police Training and Development, 2002 in Commonwealth-wide competition, as many as 50,000 FoP volunteers and an equal number of 50,000 police personnel from constable to higher ranks have been trained as on date over the past five years by the FoP Multimedia Training Centre in Chennai. The faculty who is corporate trainers fan out every year to all districts and cities and conduct workshops that train the police personnel and the FoPs in the Attitudes, Skills and Knowledge (ASK) of community policing. As many as 1000 such multimedia workshops have been conducted, unprecedented anywhere globally. The FoP multimedia Centre is virtually the world's first community policing academy.

The practical fallout of such training is manifest in cases being detected, intelligence being shared, conflict resolution, law and order problems being resolved or contained or pre-empted. Apart from these benefits, the

3,00,000 FoPs act as force multiplier. FoP is a hearts and minds strategy and not a mere eyes and ears one, hence it also leads to more enlightened and active citizenry. Following 9/11, the USA turned its attention on Homeland Security and largely neutralised the exposed vulnerabilities by a slew of measures, all coming under the umbrella of Homeland Security.

Should we not, as one of the world's largest powers with our vulnerabilities exposed by 26-29/11, also create a Department of Homeland Security. Homeland Security has effectively prevented or pre-empted any major attack within the USA after the 9/11 devastation.

At the crux of Homeland Security are the annual investments of approximately $25 billion or a quarter of the budget of the US Secret Service on developing a Citizens' Intelligence Network, quite akin to the FoP concept that could create an architecture of intelligence and information flow right from rag pickers to the super rich who were largely the victims and targets in the most recent attacks in Aamchi Mumbai.

The need of the nation is a national but rational policy on Homeland Security that works on security issues, generates innumerable asymmetric war-game scenarios on a constant basis and not just when an attack takes place.

While Mumbaikars and Indians at large would like to affirm that enough is enough, from the perspective of the subterranean forces of darkness, enough is never enough. The more spectacular the assault is, the greater the adrenalin kick it gives the terrorists and their masterminds, be it national, subnational or non-state. This implies that while these words are being typed out, some of these forces are out there planning another attack, more determined, more lethal and spectacular than the last one.

Such a reality calls for the entire opposing forces of the security dragnet and people everywhere need to be impregnated with a Factor X line of thinking. It also implies the formation of X Cells in cities, corporate organisations and police as well as other security forces. The X Cells need to constantly review security apparatus, procedures and processes, generate possible creative threat visualisations and take steps to counter them.

Talking to a former US police chief soon after 26/11, I learnt that the crux of the anti-terror apparatus in the USA is the SWAT team. Every town and city has a highly equipped and trained SWAT Team (20 to 50 personnel available round the clock depending on the size of the community). She was surprised that a town of the size of Mumbai does not have such a SWAT team.

These SWAT teams who can be mobilised even from neighbouring precincts under mutual assistance agreements, have equipments like ballistic shields, rocket propellers that enable them to move with sufficient protection towards the threat X and neutralise it as soon as possible. To wait for the army to reach would invariably mean delay and the tactics of containment as opposed to directly neutralising the threat.

Therefore, the suggestions to fight terror are threefold:

a) Extend Friends of Police to all states in the country
b) Set up SWAT teams in all towns, installations and cities

c) Set up X cells in corporate houses, security forces to assess, predict and neutralize planned terrorist assaults.

Another milestone crossed at the time of writing is that 5.5 million private security personnel across the country have been empowered to be Friends of Police augmenting at one stroke the scarce security resources of the country as well as transforming the role, esteem, reach and effectiveness of private security agencies and their personnel.

13

Low Intensity Conflicts

AP Maheshwari, IPS

Not very long ago, there was a newspaper report to the effect that tribals in Chattisgarh are facing the terror brunt from all the three sides—the Naxals, the security forces and the locally sponsored self-defence groups. It may not be an absolute truth but on the contrary is also not liable to be completely discarded. Nevertheless, it throws open a big question before all of us. The question, which is valid across the globe, hits the basic premise, 'what are we looking for?' Is there anything important for our security forces to know while undertaking operations against the target groups?

The best way to visualize what could be wrong in our approach is to step into the shoes of the local habitats. We would then soon realize that it is not only relevant to ascertain 'who is our enemy' it is equally crucial to demarcate 'who is not our enemy'. This holds good for all those conflict zones on the internal security grid where the local populace lives in the constant fear of a 'terror triangle'. Technologically exported global terror, a major cause of concern to all, already keeps the common man bewildered about what may be the next untoward threat lurking in the dark, and waiting to raise its ugly head the next moment. And as if that is not enough, the known 'counter-terror sleuths' too, at times, leave behind a chilling impact that cuts across the bones of these masses, notwithstanding the pressures of the self defence groups that they have to live with. Thus, one is left really confused in this world of the 'known unknowns' and 'unknown unknowns'. A significant 'credibility gap' is thereby constantly perpetuated.

The security forces, as part of their compartmentalized notions, generally develop two types of cognitions towards the public in such conflict zones, either in terms of they being a part of terror support structure or a potent conduit of any information about them. It is beyond these particularities, that we have to understand the concept of 'Humam Terrain Mapping'. Secondly, it is also in sharp contrast to the 'physical terrain mapping' which otherwise forms a part of the 'learnings' of the security forces for dominating the area to reverse the lose-win situation.

Mere physical terrain mapping, however, is not sufficient. This aspect, however, assumes significance due to the sizable number of armed forces that are sent into the conflict zones to countervail the violence. The forces which are trained to undertake surgical operations on the detection of the 'enemy' often fail to differentiate 'who is not an enemy'. During the unguided operations, therefore, many more casualties of trust, goodwill and hopes find their way which totally negate the impact of whatever progress we would have made in sanitizing the given area. It is here that we must relearn our lessons when we are not being humane towards the 'non-enemies'. The way one analyses the geographical terrains in the area of operation in terms of safe routes or alternate routes, IED prone areas or sanitized segments, contours of the local camouflage etc; similarly one has to conduct the human terrain mapping (HTM). This appears essential for two reasons. One, the enemy is well blended in the general populace and non-segregation may lead to avoidable torture and thereby the alienation of the 'non-enemy'. Two, the forces would fail to achieve 'value-based' performance which has a propensity to further widen the credibility gaps in the system.

'Value-based' performance should not be taken to mean the creation of 'sources' for effective operational results. Creation of 'sources' in these conflicts zones is altogether a different ball game where a person is approached by the forces or agencies with a definite motive and his weaknesses are exploited for a favourable operational outcome. Mostly such people are spoilt professionals who have the potential to make the crossover. Human terrain mapping is not concerned with a mere knowledge of such people for operational intelligence. Rather, it takes a pragmatic approach to 'cultural intelligence' about the local people so that the 'non-enemies' are not confused with the real 'enemies' or vice versa. We must try to know the local people as intimately as a mother knows her child. We would then be able to undertake the various psycho-behavioural operations to make a mark and indirectly wipe out the 'enemy'. Needless to say that none of the sides in this dangerous game of fierce guns and explosives can survive without the public support, be it covert or overt. Optimising the proper use of the support base of the local people, not for operational intelligence, but for meaningful intervention and stabilization holds the key to success in today's era of proxy war. One may also have to think in terms of 'politico-security' to usher in the democratic process so that people have an alternate viable option to the 'terror dictats'. Understanding behavioural dynamics of the local population, given the sociocultural and the economic constraints, is sine qua non for peace to return pronto and that too with desired stability. Like in the body, the holistics of the system too need to be well understood before the surgeon decides where to cut and how deep to cut, notwithstanding the past and future sustenance of the concerned patient.

Hence, the HTM concepts necessitate multifaceted sociocultural interface in the region with the help of experts dealing with various facets of life. It may range from a political worker to the social or human rights activists; psychologists, doctors, lawyers, musicians, playwriters, journalists, historians, etc. This leads us to the need for an advisory team consisting of the above in the given zone of conflict to guide the captains of the security forces working in that area so that they don't miss the mark. Physical security, in fact, would tend to become redundant if carried out without 'cultural security' where a person loves to sustain himself along with congnitively nurtured 'self-emotions'. War of perceptions is, nonetheless, far more potent than a war of guns in this democratized world of ours where each human being deserves a humane treatment, much less the essential social respect.

It is not difficult for the police chiefs or the commanders of the paramilitary forces to get attuned to the HTM. They are well aware of the importance of the 'Human Mapping' of the soldiers they lead in order to ensure that they be counted amongst effective leaders. A well considered extension of the human terrain approach shall assist them to lead well in the 'physical terrain' they are asked to operate within.

In the social setup where people are not alienated with local administration and systems of self-governance are more or less in place with a participative mode, we have been trying various models of community policing and drawing synergies out of the holistic efforts. In low intensity war zones, till we reach such a point, HTM provides an effective tool. Since 'security' and 'development' in these areas remain a part of the vicious circle of abnormality, one being taken as an excuse for the other and vice versa, security forces have to take a lead. The concepts of area dominance have to shift from inorganic physical terrains to organic human profiles.

14

Combating Terrorism

Dhirendra Singh, IAS

No other subject has attracted so much heated debate as the one on special laws to combat terrorism (organized crime, transnational and interstate crime are added to the list only in the context of a Federal Investigation Agency). Considering that India provides for capital punishment, the question is not so much of stringent punishment (or deterrence) but the means to prevent, investigate and bring to book the perpetrators of such heinous crimes. The debate accordingly centres on matters like preventive detention, bail provisions, admissibility of confessions before the police, use of intercepts and the burden of proof etc. In short, such special laws are tested against the template of ordinary jurisprudence and the criminal justice system of countries following the common law principles.

The mass of literature on the subject comprising newspaper articles; interviews; research publications and books would give the impression that a majority of the people (or at least those voicing their opinion publicly) do not favour special laws as they are wont to categorize them, as draconian laws.

There is good reason for the seemingly lesser number of public advocates for stringent laws. Most of them are part of the establishment, and for them it is not so much an intellectual debate, but one which impacts on their profession directly and in a large number of cases with deadly effect. They have a voice in those closed chambers where decisions are taken and where the political executive has to think carefully about its responsibilities to keep the society and state together. Over the years, emerging crimes have been met by specially tailored laws and the fact that so many have remained on the statute books for so long is testimony to their legitimacy. Obviously, those who are interested in reversing the trend need to bring in better firepower, and constantly seek to grab the headlines. It is they who have to muster courage and make their voices heard. Those who have to maintain the status quo or just wait patiently for events to unfold on a predictable path merely need to ensure that their holding positions are not breached.

Those in favour of having more stringent laws point towards the several such legislation on drug possession and trafficking; on preventive detention; and on many earlier special laws on internal security (viz. Maintenance of Internal Security Act; Terrorist and Disruptive Practices Act; Prevention of Terrorism Act) and similar such legislation in other countries especially the US (which after 9/11 has completely revamped its legal institutional and criminal justice system to deal with terrorist acts). Misuse they aver is inherent in all systems but countries like India which have an independent judiciary need not fear as judicial review is a balancing force to executives over-reach. Moreover, if this argument is accepted, even ordinary laws being misused would lose credibility. Terrorists are not ordinary criminals and their motivation, training and methods and callous disregard for human life need to be matched by special laws which must differ from ordinary laws to the same extent as the terrorist crimes differ from ordinary crimes, if the State has to have the remotest chance of bringing the guilty to justice. Ideological indoctrination, trans-border training and escape havens, access to enormous funds emanating from illegal activities; extreme motivation of some individuals and groups who are willing to sacrifice their own lives; re-emergence of banned outfits under different names; and above all the covert support of sovereign states make the fight against terrorism extremely difficult. Any soft attitude towards perpetrators of such crimes would be a sign of weakness and the descent from a 'soft state' to a 'failed state' is steep and fast.

Attention is also invited to a subtle psychological warfare being conducted wittingly or unwittingly. Mistakes by security agencies are grossly magnified and in many cases even legitimate action is wrongly characterized and criticism of heavy handedness levelled, the most frequent being that of human rights violations. The armed forces are caught on the horns of a dilemma. Trained and motivated to take on a uniformed adversary of another sovereign state they are required to fight civilians, many of them own nationals sheltering amongst a body of peaceful citizens, attacking clandestinely and then melting into inaccessible terrain or amongst the populace. Laws enacted to protect them from frivolous charges are constantly being attacked by the local population as well as by the growing number of intellectuals who would like them to be repealed. What to speak of being commended for gallantry, they fight under fear of being hauled up for violations of human rights and wonder if this is what they had signed up for. What is most galling to the security apparatus is that many activists and intellectuals have inadvertently fallen into the trap laid by terrorist organizations and with their sympathetic views and espousement of their cause lend them a legitimacy they so fervently crave.

Terrorism and transnational crime because of their global imprint, require a response which can come only through global and regional efforts with consensus on critical issues including definition, punishment, extradition and information sharing. Action on many of these can come only through statutory backing incorporating such consensus. There is therefore no escape from special laws especially for India which has suffered from terrorist activity for many decades and which shares borders with countries which aid and abet such activities.

Opponents of special laws base their arguments on (a) proven inefficacy of special laws to tackle terrorism (b) the deleterious effect they have on the investigation agency which gets accustomed to short-cuts and slipshod investigation and (c) their widespread misuse by targeting minorities and gross human rights violations. The panacea they say lies not in more stringent laws but by better intelligence gathering, policing, investigation, successful prosecution and by concerted action by the state and society to address the underlying causes of such terrorist acts.

Statistics they say confirm that special laws have had no effect except to swell the number of lawful citizens who have been subjected to unnecessary detention and harassment and thereby harbour a sense of guidance. Out of 77,000 people arrested under TADA, 72,000 were released without a charge. Of those prosecuted only 1.8% were convicted. The same is true of the United States which claims to have an astounding success post 9/11. *The Washington Post* quoting Justice Department figures says that there have been only 39 convictions under special laws, the rest 200 were found guilty of minor crimes like violation of immigration laws. Most terrorism investigations did not find al-Qaeda links but rather those with narcotic cartels, Rwandan war criminals, supporters of Palestinian causes and likewise. Many suspects were taken into custody out of malice. The UK Home Office figures of 2007 indicate that just 40 out of 1200 suspects held on terrorism charges were convicted. Most of the suspects were released without trial. As regards prevention the record too is dismal. Attacks on Akshardham, Parliament and the J&K Assembly took place when POTA was in force. Restrictive measures especially those undertaken in parts of the country, convert themselves into oppressive practices and alienate vast sections of the local people. The same views continue to be expressed even after the amendments made to the Unlawful

Activities Prevention Act in the aftermath of the November 2008, Mumbai terrorist attack. The amendments it is said were a reaction to the "jingoism and muscle flexing in the media and on the streets."

What is needed is not special laws but better policing. There is no substitute to a professional, well-trained and motivated force. It should be supported by adequate infrastructure, like scientific aids and forensic laboratories; an efficient intelligence apparatus and a comprehensive data base.

Relaxed rules of evidence rather than aiding prosecution provide the incentive for lax investigation, and to cut corners, more so when the onus is on the accused to prove his innocence. Stringent laws do not make for efficient policemen. They are the knee-jerk reactions of ineffective governments and take away a great many of the protections which ordinary laws give to ordinary people.

However, it is in their defence of the oppressed especially targeted minorities that the advocates of the ordinary criminal justice system bring forth their most cogent arguments. A corrupt criminal justice system if armed with draconian laws will only victimize the socially and politically marginalized. They are counter productive as they aggravate political disaffection and alienate citizens because of repression. POTA added to the woes of thousands of innocent Muslims, who were harassed and persecuted by an inept and vindictive police force which made them scapegoats for its failure to nab the real culprits. Many have gone on to say that state repression is worse than terrorism. "In a ruthless, repressive state where dissent is disallowed and civil rights are cast aside, where you can be jailed as a terrorist for protesting against extra-judicial killings, terrorism may seem like a lesser evil." It is not as if in the US or UK such laws have been accepted without dissent. When the Patriot Act in the US was being debated, dissenting voices were raised in the *NY Times, Washington Post* and the *Philadelphia Inquirer.* There was a sustained campaign in the UK by human rights activists under the banner of "charge or release" when the government sought to increase the remand period from 28 days to 42 days. They have succeeded as of now, as the Lords rejected the bill. These views have wide acceptance even in societies where the police have a better reputation of honesty and fair play. In contrast the police in India are considered to be more corrupt, inefficient, unethical and politically pliable. Justice, say the advocates of this school, does not mean subversion of the principles of liberal jurisprudence but greater and uniform compliance with them. If a person is willing to confess what is the problem in taking him before a magistrate?

Even though the Supreme Court, it is admitted, upheld the constitutional validity of the special laws, it warned that: "If Human Rights are violated in the process of combating terrorism, it will be self-defeating. Terrorism often thrives where Human Rights are violated ..." Stringent bail provisions are also not the norm. The 14-day remand in India is very high compared to most other countries. Only the UK has a remand period of 28 days in its terror laws. On the other hand, Australia has 12, Turkey/Ireland seven, France six, Spain/Russia five, Italy four, US/Germany/New Zealand two and Canada only one. And lastly attacking the best defence of the protagonists of stringent anti-terror laws who say that in a vibrant democracy excesses are widely publicised and redress sought from the judiciary, it is said that experience has shown the apathy of the law makers and the guardians of liberty. Looking at the dwindling number of lawmakers who participated in the Parliamentary debates on TADA between 1985-1993 it is commented that "the sensitivity of MPs at the deprivation of basic rights of citizens is becoming dulled." And the record of the judiciary has also not been very bright. Since the constitutional validity of such laws has been upheld the detainee has a much tougher battle. Chief Justice A.N. Ray's remark in the well quoted ADM (Jabalpur) 1976 case that "liberty itself was the gift of the law and may by the law be forfeited or abridged" has become the rallying point of opponents of special laws and their frustration at the helplessness of the Courts.

Rather than allowing the debate to be hijacked by the two lobbies, saner voices are calling for the best minds in the country represented by the Law Commission and the National Human Rights Commission to advise on the matter. The question is whether under present circumstances in the wider public and national interest individual Human Rights safeguarded under our Constitution do really need to be sacrificed at the altar of another fierce anti-terrorist law, a law which will certainly be misused by some States for political ends, as was POTA and TADA before it?

Regardless of what school one belongs to, the enactment of laws must follow the Constitutional dictates. They are a reflection of the majority view or in some cases, a consensus view prevailing in Parliament. Thus the legitimacy of laws cannot be questioned and dissatisfaction must remain till the lawmakers choose to repeal or amend them. The debate therefore on the procedural aspects will continue. On the punishment having a deterrent effect there is no great difference of opinion. The efficacy or otherwise of capital punishment is not confined to special laws alone. The only conclusion that can be reached is that each nation must at all times answer for itself the question of how a balance is to be struck between the need to maintain the security of the nation and its obligation to safeguard individual liberties guaranteed by the Constitution, especially those given to the minorities. In a democratic polity such laws would continue to be judged against the ordinary laws and deviations would need to be justified with valid arguments based on extreme necessity, effectiveness and safeguards to protect against wrongdoing.

India is not alone to be confronted with the dilemma of finding a balance between security and freedom. It is a responsibility which must be shared by all: the legislative, the judiciary and public opinion. One of the legal innovations which is attracting the attention of intellectuals is that of "proportionality". Infringements of rights are subjected to several tests. Germany's Constitutional Court has used this principle in a number of landmark cases to find a right balance. This and similar other innovations need to be studied. Public debate needs to be steered to finding a via media as at present it is highly polarized.

Not all demands are to make it easier for the investigation agency. There are many who seek to bring about fundamental changes in the criminal justice system.

Since they do not seek to enhance the powers of the police, they should be more acceptable. It has been argued that the "right to silence" which is an inviolable rule of the Indian justice system is not so much a right but a privilege and in heinous and terrorist related crimes it is the obligation of the accused to assist the judge in the discovery of truth. A positive obligation must be cast on the accused to assist the investigation and if the Court so requires to give evidence. The aim of "discovery of the truth" as against finding proof of guilt as practised in the inquisitorial system of justice (where magistrates guide investigation and prosecution) is more suited to trials in terrorist related cases. The Malimath Committee Report of March 2003 has made important recommendations on reorientation of the criminal justice system and this need to be revisited. Some procedures being adopted by countries like the US or UK could also be studied. They relate to bail before charge (with those on bail being electronically tagged to prevent escape); and post charge questioning. The fundamental principle is that in terrorist related and suchlike crimes the rights of Society and justice for the victims too must be addressed. Special laws which cover these aspects and bring about a fundamental change in the justice delivery system and actually empower the judiciary and not the police, would not only be more helpful in the conviction of terror accused but at the same time be more acceptable to different sections of society.

There is another and more subtle reason for laws to be framed carefully. There is general acceptance now that a two-fold assault needs to be made on terrorism; one is by means of the bullet which does physical damage, the other by influencing his mind and heart. The latter is of lasting significance, for ultimately it is in the mind and hearts that the battle has to be won. For every Abdullah Azam and Syed Qutb one can find an al-Ghazali and Ibn al-Sayyid. Deoband has set the trend to disassociate itself from the wrong interpretation given to the Quranic teachings. The moderates amongst Muslims and Hindus are asserting themselves. It is also heartening that the youth in the country are apt to support a moderate line of action, a stark contrast to many of the older generation who are wont to take a hard line. The laws must in some manner reflect this belief and support the moderates as salvation lies only on that route.

Regardless of what shape the laws would take, there is unanimity in the belief that the instrumentality of special laws are of no great benefit if they are not in the hands of an efficient law and order machinery which has the confidence and respect of the people and whose credibility is not in doubt. It is this aspect which holds the key to the fight against terror and organized crime.

Irrespective of the stand taken on special laws, protagonists on both sides call for building an efficient intelligence, and investigative institutional mechanism. Each side builds its case on different assumptions. Those for stringent laws say that these are to aid the police which have to match their skills with those of the perpetrators of such crimes. Those against stringent laws say that what is required is efficient force and not stringent laws. In this regard numerous suggestions have been made on revamping the police establishment. In-house discussions amongst police officers, public debates, parliamentary discussions and court directives, as well as numerous reports of the Commissions set up for the purpose have thrown up a slew of recommendations. What needs to be done is acceptance and honest implementation. Building credibility is, however, something more than bringing about efficiency. Credibility is a matter of trust and willing support. An efficient but ruthless institution does not have such public support. One of the most forceful arguments against bringing about stringent laws and placing them at the disposal of the police is that the police in India unlike in the UK and the US has little credibility and is considered as untrustworthy and highly compromised. These attributes of the police are ascribed to the colonial hangover. Many of the ills of the system are because the police do not provide "sensitive and people friendly policing", as the system was designed to be loyal and subservient to the rulers of the moment. Accountability to the law was not a part of the ordinary policeman's psyche. This resulted in several malpractices like non-registration of complaints, or even if they condescended to do so by distorting facts or not following prescribed procedures; torture in custody; corruption and partisan behaviour. The poor and disadvantaged became the most common victim of this attitude. The position becomes worse when the police is armed with powers under special laws. Whereas it is expected that implementation of the host of recommendations could bring about reforms in the system, human rights activists remain chary of the outcome. According to them they do not address the core concerns of accountability of the police considering the widespread abuse of powers.

Political interference according to them is not the main concern of most people though it remains at the top of the agenda of the police hierarchy. The oversight of the members of the society should be made more effective and the law should be amended to enable quick decisions on prosecution of policemen accused of violating human rights under the guise of performing their duty. The record of detentions and prosecutions under special legislation has grossly undermined the reputation of police force and alienated them from large sections of society especially amongst the Muslims. Considering the historical origins of the community in India and the fact that they are as much a part of the soil as the majority community and that their numbers are large there is no way in which in a democratic polity such as ours, their alienation can be disregarded. In fact looking at recent trends wherein homespun youth have taken to the path of terrorism, with or without outside support, the matter has assumed serious proportions. The most vicious enemy is that within and extreme care would need to be taken to isolate it as a thin line separates alienation from revolt. It is not only minority sensitivities which need to be considered. Regardless of what the actual cases may be, an argument is put forth that the police are being used to target organizations of the majority Hindu community only to demonstrate that terrorism has no faith and can be nurtured in almost any community. Such beliefs have very serious portents for a culturally diverse country.

The usual answers on how to build credibility is to allow the police to function professionally without political interference and allow them to implement the rule of law. Once they are allowed to do so, they would prove themselves and trust would closely follow. Perhaps this is how most police forces, which are held up as examples have evolved, but in India few are willing to take the chance. Any institution which is armed with punitive powers cannot be left to internal controls alone and to say that there should be no executive control outside the hierarchy would not be realistic. It is also argued that the constitutional mandate to govern cannot be disregarded by the political executive. Regardless of the low esteem in which the people hold most politicians they are still the most accessible body of people. An uninformed hierarchy, not accessible, armed with stringent punitive powers, and given the power to investigate and also to prosecute and yet not be subject to day-to-day control would not be acceptable. Moreover there are many instances of the moderating influence of the political executive on misplaced professional enthusiasm. In Prakash Singh versus Union of India the Supreme Court stated: "The commitment, devotion and accountability of the police have to be only to the Rule of Law. The supervision and control have to be such that ensure that the police serve the people without any regard, whatsoever, to the status and position of any person while investigating a crime or taking preventive measures". The current debate is hence on how this accountability to the law has to be enforced. Whereas protagonists from amongst the police would favour a complete independence in most matters, proponents of civil and minority rights do not see any merit in completely severing the police from political (meaning people's representatives) control. The balance, it is said, can be achieved by a legal delineation of powers and responsibilities of the political executive and the police administration. The Commonwealth Human Rights Initiative has been suggesting that India can in its proposed comprehensive revised Police Act incorporate some of the salutary provisions of New Zealand's legislation which has addressed this issue. Apart from such a clear delineation of responsibilities by statute the police establishment and the procedures which guide its functioning need a revamp. A mere tinkering of the establishment with its basic features intact will not make a difference. A radical makeover only could convince the people that the government means business.

It would be pertinent to flip the coin at this juncture, and for a moment ponder on what the policeman has to say. He is a much harassed person. He performs important functions but is held in low esteem. The extent of lawbreaking by ordinary citizens is appalling. The most cited example is of violation of traffic rules. Even the most educated and well heeled do not hesitate to break them. When accosted they are quick to point out to their connections. But this is at the lower end of the rule breaking spectrum. It is when a leadership emerges and harnesses the energies of lumpen elements that the policeman's nightmare begins. Bandhs are called and enforced, whole cities are sometimes besieged with roads and railway networks blocked (and damaged) until the demands are met. Compromises are brought about and the lawbreakers many a time emerge as heroes of one cause or another. The criminal justice system designed to take care of individuals or small gangs is helpless against hundreds or even thousands of otherwise law abiding citizens breaking the law. All this has resulted in extreme demoralization of the police force. The ordinary policeman's story is hardly ever told. There are many who would like to do their job honestly and faithfully but soon give up. In countries which are held up as examples, policemen do not have to contend with such mass scale violations of the law. The law in those countries is enforced regardless of the social standing or office held of the lawbreaker. And this more than anything else has built the image of the law enforcer, and given him the respect that is his due. If major challenges of law and order and security are to be met, then the Indian policeman must have an image makeover.

Two ways are suggested: The first an administrative mechanism having a bearing on the qualitative aspects of the individual and the second a legislative measure. Much of the lack of credibility is because of the experience of individuals who visit police stations for help of any kind or those who go to register complaints. It is generally believed that the police are lackadaisical and inefficient and unhelpful. The stereotype of the policeman shown in Bollywood films and now on the TV is not without any substance. In rural India even today most cases are settled without the intervention of the police or the judicial system, The solution lies in upgrading the educational requirement for selection to police services. It is the single most effective method of enhancing the status of a public functionary. No other state authority has been vested with such enormous powers and yet whose educational requirements have been kept at such low levels. There are only police officers in the US and UK forces and no 'policemen' as understood in India. In a way we would be only recognizing the ground reality. Most applicants for the Delhi Police are graduates. There are two ways of going about this, either by making a graduate degree as the minimum qualification or by recruiting at a younger age and then providing a 3 to 4 year training programme with a graduate degree at the end, as is done for NDA cadets. Obviously, the pay scales of such officers would need to be suitably enhanced. The consequent rise in the expenditure because of such an up-gradation would be a small price to pay for the benefits that are bound to accrue. This recommendation would only apply to the intelligence and civil police and not to the armed police which are not involved in investigation and regular public contact. With this training and qualification the policemen would be turned into officers, and once this status is conferred on them public recognition of the change would follow. A radical break from the past would be made. The Committee appointed by the ministry of home affairs to draft a model Police Act to replace the 1861 Act, has made such a suggestion. This suggestion has also been endorsed by the second Administrative Reforms Commission in its fifth report of June 2007. Such a step would also remove some of the basic objections to having and placing more stringent laws at their disposal. The second suggestion involves a conceptual change in the criminal justice system. The broad principles of 'separation of powers' and 'checks and balance' has always been used to limit executive tyranny. In the criminal justice system a separation of the executive from the judiciary has been affected. The prosecutor will not be the judge. Likewise we need to go a step further and completely isolate investigation from the power to file charges and prosecute. One of the main causes for the alienation of the police and the fear they instil amongst the common man has been their power to file charges, even though investigation has been shoddy, relying on the slow criminal justice system to keep people behind bars whilst cases drag on for years. Commenting even on the powers of arrest the Supreme Court has deprecated the practice of arrest on frivolous grounds. The Court has warned that not only it deprives the citizen of his liberty but the mere fact of arrest is a slur on his honour which is not easily removed. Following the Supreme Court's judgements and the 177th report (December 2001) of the Law Commission, the Code of Criminal Procedure was rightly amended in 2008 stipulating that for cognizable offences punishable with a maximum imprisonment of less than seven years, arrests should be made only against the existence of "credible information" or a "reasonable complaint". In most cases a notice of appearance should suffice. The jails are mainly populated by under-trials and stories keep emerging of persons having spent decades in jail for petty crimes in which a mere fine would have sufficed. The position is the worst in anti-terror laws where review committees (the latest being those which looked into POTA cases) have found little ground for prosecution in most cases. The National Crime Records Bureau of the ministry of home affairs in its publication "Crime in India 2007" states that the number of persons arrested in the country in 2007 was 27,80,559 under IPC cases and 40,87,246 under special and local laws making a total of nearly 68 lakhs. But reverting to the power to file a chargesheet, unfortunately it has become an incentive for shoddy investigation. Filing of the charge sheet is considered the end of a successful investigation and failure to convict can then be laid at the doors of inept public prosecutors or unreliable witnesses. Good examples are the system of the District Attorney in the US (aided by the plea bargaining procedures) and the Crown Prosecution Service in the UK. That prosecution would come only after the application of a legally trained and independent (of the investigative machinery) mind to the evidence thrown-up by the investigation brings enormous comfort to the citizen. He is then more prone to cooperate with the police. Moreover, the prosecutors would look into the loopholes of the investigation at the right time and guide the investigation machinery based on what they assess is the probability of getting a conviction. In the case of terror laws it has helped in other ways also. Usually, the principle in ordinary jurisprudence is to convict only when guilt has been proven to the hilt and the more serious the charge the more stringent the test of guilt. Charging authorities have to base their judgement on "the basis of realistic prospect of conviction." A dilution of this principle would be more acceptable if it is adopted by an independent authority rather than the police. In the UK the Crown Prosecution Service (CPS) which since 2004 has been given the power to charge, has in terror cases, adopted the principle of "reasonable suspicion". This is a lower threshold but has had public acceptability. Even here the head of the CPS Sir Ken MacDonald has admitted that the practice could lead to a "grave infringement of the liberty of the individual". Parliamentary Committees have suggested that this practice be codified and given statutory basis. The fear that a completely independent prosecution service may make the task of the police still more difficult is justified. This can happen at the stage of filing charges and at the trial stage. If the police could be compromised and influenced, so can the prosecution service. This is a valid argument. However, this fear must be addressed instead of jettisoning the principle viz. separation of investigation from the power to prosecute. It would be necessary to provide for proper qualifications for the prosecutors, their selection should be on the basis of well laid down criteria and procedures and they must have fixity of tenure and their independence assured. To ensure that the investigation agency is not completely ignored oversight committees need to be constituted to ensure that the prosecutor is performing its functions strictly in accordance with the law. This law should lay down the consultation process which the prosecutor must follow prior to filing of charges and later during the course of prosecution. The two agencies should work in synergy, rather than at cross purposes, to ensure that justice is done.

Index

List of Contributors

Ajit Doval is a former Director of the Intelligence Bureau (IB), India.

General S Padmanabhan is a former Chief of the Army Staff, Indian Army.

Lt Gen Kamal Davar an armoured Corps officer has been GOC Ladakh and Corps Commander, Punjab.

DS Rajan is director, Chennai Center for China Studies, Chennai.

MK Dhar is a former Joint Director, Intelligence Bureau (IB) and an specialist on Pakistan and Jihad related matters.

Dr NC Asthana is presently IG (Opertions—CRPF), Srinagar (J&K).

Lt Gen PC Katoch is a retired Director General Infomation Systems of the Indian Army and erstwhile Colonel of the Special Forces and Parachute Regiment.

Lt Gen SK Sinha is a former Governor of Jammu & Kashmir, Assam, India's Ambassador to Nepal, Vice Chief of the Indian Army and Director General of Military Intelligence.

Lt Gen DB Shekatkar is presently the Member, Governing Council for Advanced Strategic Studies, Pune.

BR Lall has been Director-General of Police, Haryana and Joint Director—Central Bureau of Investigation (CBI).

DC Pathak is a former Director of Intelligence Bureau and a former Member, National Security Advisory Board.

Dr Prateep V Philip is the Inspector General of Police, Tamil Nadu and Project Director, Friends of Police.

AP Maheshwari is an IPS officer, presently working as IGP (Law and Order), UP Police.

Dhirendra Singh retired as Union Home Secretary, Government of India.